ESCAPE OR DIE

TRUE STORIES OF YOUNG PEOPLE WHO SURVIVED THE HOLOCAUST

Ina R. Friedman

Yellow Moon Press   Boston

ISBN: 0-938756-34-6

Escape Or Die

First published by Addison-Wesley Publishing Company

Reprinted by Yellow Moon Press 1991

Text Copyright © 1982 by Ina R. Friedman

Printed in the United States of America.

For Further information contact:
Yellow Moon Press
P.O. Box 1316
Cambridge, MA 02238
(617) 776 - 2230

Acknowledgments

I should like to thank the following people for their comments and assistance during the preparation of this manuscript: Rabbi Benjamin Kahn, past executive director of B'nai B'rith International; Rabbi Eugene Lipman, Temple Sinai, Washington, D.C.; Rabbi Bernard Mehlman, Temple Israel, Brookline, Massachusetts; my son, Rabbi Ronne Friedman, Temple Israel, Brookline, Massachusetts; Judith Robbins of West Roxbury, Massachusetts, and my editor, Cyrisse Jaffee.

I am also indebted to Arnost Lustig, author and professor of Film and Literature at American University; to Dr. Elaine Shalowitz of the University of the District of Columbia, and to Jerry Rosenthal of Washington, D.C. for their suggestions. Mrs. Leah Silverstein of the Library of Congress was most helpful in locating pictorial resources. Max Rosenberg, Historian, U.S. Air Force, was kind enough to check the manuscript for historical accuracy. Mr. Franz Rogier translated various documents.

Mr. Ivor Davis, of the Nairobi Hebrew Congregation, Nairobi, Kenya; my cousin, Lilithea Singer, of Johannesburg, South Africa; Mickey and Ariel Renin of Chamadia, Israel; Mary Khyatt of Haifa, Israel; my cousins, Eli and Joseph Schweid of Jerusalem, Israel; Hil Irasquin of the Netherlands, in addition to many others, helped me in my search for those whose stories appear here.

My deepest thanks, too, to my "in-house" critic, my husband, Sam D. Starobin, for his patience and support.

Foreword

The writing of this book has been both a mission and a challenge. The stories that follow were obtained through personal interviews I conducted in Africa, Asia, Europe, and North and South America. All over the world, I knocked on doors, asking people to remember and recount their past. Strangers — who had hidden their scars for thirty-five years — shared with me the terrible paradox of their lives: outwardly, all memories of their homeland had been forgotten; yet the ache of expulsion from their countries had never vanished. In many cases, the storyteller would invite his or her children to hear, for the first time, the tale of exodus.

A total of thirty-five million individuals, civilian and military, were killed in World War II. The Holocaust of World War II is frequently thought of as the "Jewish Holocaust." While the Jews as a people, solely because of their religion, were singled out for destruction and Six Million perished, five million non-Jews were also annihilated in the death camps. These non-Jewish victims included Jehovah's Witnesses, gypsies, Social Democrats, labor leaders, theologians, atheists, and ordinary citizens who rose up to protest and to fight against the Nazis. In addition to those who were murdered, untold numbers were physically and emotionally incapacitated because of the horrors and deprivations they experienced. Millions more suffered the dangers and traumas of escape and the rebuilding of their lives in alien countries.

The selection of these particular histories, from over one hundred interviews, portrays the diversity of escape routes and destinations, and each individual's determination to rebuild his or her life. The tales cover the years 1933-1948, and with one exception, deal only with those individuals who were not sent to the concentration camps.

This book is not intended to minimize the deaths of the Six Million, and the five million non-Jews, many of whom were murdered before they were aware of the danger or were killed trying to escape. For many imprisoned in the death camps and ghettos, evading the gas chambers and firing squads was simply impossible.

I have not included stories of the Scandinavian countries since their acts of heroism are well documented. The Danes smuggled over 6000 Jews into neutral Sweden. Other nations, not represented in this collection, also aided the Jews. Bulgaria, a Balkan country, through the intercession of the Church, refused to let the Nazis deport its Jewish population. Only one story of Dutch valor is told here, yet a great number of Holland's ten million citizens took part in resistance efforts.

And individuals in many countries defied both the Nazis and their countrymen to save Jewish lives and to sabotage the enemy.

Through each of these stories runs a theme common to refugees in any time, any place: "I will survive." In an era dominated by death, to survive was to resist. Thus, while this book deals with a period of unprecedented horror, the theme is one of personal triumph. It is a survivor's book, universal in its message — the striving for life, against all odds and at all costs.

Some of the names have been changed to protect individual privacy, but the facts are unaltered.

Despite the warnings of friends who thought the writing of these stories would be a depressing experience, I have found the task exhilarating. My thanks to those who welcomed me into their homes and did not let me leave a stranger.

> Ina R. Friedman
> Brookline, Massachusetts
> Chillicothe, Ohio
> 1981

A WORD ABOUT THIS NEW EDITION OF ESCAPE OR DIE

With the appearance of my second book on the Holocaust, THE OTHER VICTIMS: FIRST PERSON STORIES OF NON–JEWS PERSECUTED BY THE NAZIS (Houghton Mifflin), there has been a demand on the part of educators, librarians, Holocaust centers and parents for a paperback edition of its predecessor, ESCAPE OR DIE: TRUE STORIES OF YOUNG PEOPLE WHO SURVIVED THE HOLOCAUST, for use in the home and in the classroom.

ESCAPE OR DIE deals chiefly with young men and women who were persecuted solely because they were Jews. THE OTHER VICTIMS: FIRST PERSON STORIES OF NON–JEWS PERSECUTED BY THE NAZIS presents the stories of non–Jews who were murdered or enslaved during the Holocaust for racial and religious reasons. Together, the two books delineate the affect of totalitarianism on all segments of society.

The introductory pieces that precede each personal story provide the political and social background of the times. The reader can then relate on a personal basis to the young men and women whose lives were threatened by the Nazis.

In the original edition of ESCAPE OR DIE: TRUE STORIES OF YOUNG PEOPLE WHO SURVIVED THE HOLOCAUST. I had to omit several stories from among the many I had collected in my travels. Because a great many more people found sanctuary in South America than in India, I have taken the liberty of substituting the story, "Beneath the Earth", for the Austrian story in the first edition.

"Beneath the Earth" reflects the conditions in which thousands of refugees who fled to South America found themselves. It is also the story of a teenager's determination to establish a place for himself in a physically and emotionally hostile environment. Like the other stories in the book, it underscores the human will to survive.

I am indebted to Robert Smyth, the publisher of the Yellow Moon Press, for issuing this new edition.

Introduction

A few hours after the Nazis invaded Poland, Wolf Goldberg and his family of ten slipped over the border into Russia. When asked why he had reacted and escaped so quickly, he gave three reasons:

- *When one Jew is slapped, I am slapped.*
- *I made my money myself; I can afford to lose it.*
- *When there are two paths — one leading to life, the other to death — I choose life.*

Most Eastern European Jews (Lithuanian, Ukrainian, Polish, Estonian) did not have the luxury of choice. Some did flee to Russia, choosing to face unknown dangers, but there was virtually no opportunity for Jews in Eastern Europe to escape the Nazis. Soon after Hitler invaded Poland, Jews in Eastern Europe were rounded up and exterminated in mass shootings or gassed in specially built vans. Those who were not immediately executed were herded into ghettos and then sent to concentration camps.

Jews of Western and Central Europe (Germany, Austria, France, the Netherlands, Belgium), on the other hand, read about or experienced Hitler's threats against Jews all during the 1930s. Many Jews in Germany, in particular, were aware of the serious growth of anti-Semitism, but ignored the danger. They were convinced that this "temporary madness" would soon be over.

"Jews are indispensable to Germany," they insisted. "We have seen many Hitlers in our history, and we have outlasted them."

Realists, like Wolf Goldberg, held no such illusions about Hitler. They did not allow material possessions to bind them to a birthplace that rejected them. Many German and Austrian Jews who could have fled in the 1930s refused to do so, declaring, "Our fate is with our fatherland." Others committed suicide rather than endure the disgrace of exile. Jews in other countries felt safe and protected from Hitler's madness. By the time they acknowledged the danger, all escape routes were closed.

By 1938, however, after the round-up of Crystal Night, an increasing number of Jews understood the necessity of escape. Ordinary people, in their search for refuge and survival, risked unknown destinations and endured primitive sanctuaries. The philosopher became a tin miner in Bolivia; the scholar, a sheep herder in Australia; the pianist sold stockings door-to-door in America to keep her family alive; the shoemaker hid in a frozen hole among the mud flats of

Lithuania. They, like so many others, refused to surrender their right to a future.

Their stories, then, are more than tales of escape. They are personal testaments: of the eternal will of the Jewish people to survive; of the covenant between man and God and between Christian and Jew. The people in these stories display enormous courage and ingenuity. Their survival is their legacy.

My thanks to Frans Rogier for translating the Dutch and German documents and to all those who provided documents and photographs for this book, including:

pages 7,12	Arthur Kahn
pages 9, 34, 44, 59, 93, 96 100, 101	National Archives
page 19	Leo Baeck Institute, New York City
pages 20-21, 23	Eric Pollitzer, Hempstead, New York
pages 26-27	Manny Gale
page 51	Ivor Davis
page 117	Memorial du Martyr Juif Inconu, Paris, France
page 139	Rabbi Eugene Lipman
pages 108, 112, 113	Baroness Elie de Rothschild

Contents

GERMANY

The Jews were not newcomers to Germany. They arrived with Julius Caesar and settled in Germany long before the various tribes, such as the Goths and the Franks — the "aryan" race Hitler claimed to be true Germans and a "Master" race.

The Jews were a unique people. Throughout centuries of ignorance in Europe, every male Jew was expected to learn how to read. Learning among Christians was generally restricted to priests and a few nobles.

Thus, Jews were equipped with the basic skills for carrying on business and trade. In the eighth century, Jews managed Charlemagne's household and supplied his armies. However, throughout the Middle Ages and the Renaissance, anti-Semitism was encouraged by the Church and state. By the seventeenth century, most German towns had expelled the Jews. However, because of their business skills, many Jews were permitted to remain at the royal courts or eventually return to cities and towns.

By 1800 there were Jewish communities throughout the various German states. When they were granted citizenship in 1871, they became prominent in every area of German culture.

During World War I, 96,000 Jews fought for the Kaiser, and 12,000 died on the battlefields. Nevertheless, when Germany lost the war, the Germans, in need of a scapegoat, blamed the Jews: "The Jews are our disgrace."

Adolph Hitler rose to power in the 1920s. His autobiography, *Mein Kampf*, stated, "Germany's final objective must unswervingly be the removal of Jews altogether."

In 1933, Germany turned against native-born Jews. With chilling efficiency, the Nazi-controlled Parliament passed one restrictive measure after another, each designed to deprive Jews of their rights as citizens and choke off their economic and social freedom.

At first, these laws caused humiliation and inconvenience: a Jewish family could no longer enjoy a glass of wine at Krantzler's; Jewish doctors were denied hospital privileges; Jewish lawyers could no longer practice. All Jewish civil servants and school teachers were dismissed from their jobs, and Jewish schools were boycotted. Marriages between Jews and Gentiles had to be annulled.

Soon the restrictions became a matter of life and death. Jews, and those with liberal political beliefs, vanished behind the doors of the Gestapo headquarters and were never seen again. The cafes and parks, the Staatsopera and theaters all displayed signs proclaiming: "No Jews and Dogs Allowed."

One-third of Germany's 500,000 Jews left Germany, but the majority could not bring themselves to believe what they read in the newspapers and saw on the streets.

It was not until November 9, 1938, Crystal Night, that the German Jews finally realized that they had only two choices: escape or death.

Crystal Night was an "unplanned," national pogrom (riot) that destroyed 76 synagogues and damaged more than one hundred others. Thirty-six Jews were killed, and 815 shops and 171 homes were demolished. Between 20,000 and 30,000 Jews were arrested and sent to concentration camps.

The Nazis had forbidden the local police to interfere with these "spontaneous" anti-Jewish demonstrations. Violence against the Jews was, in fact, carefully planned. Incredibly, a fine of one billion marks was levied against the Jewish community as "atonement payment" for the damage caused by Crystal Night — damage that had been inflicted *on* the Jews, not by them.

Jews desperately tried to obtain visas to emigrate; thousands eventually escaped with or without them. Eighteen thousand Jews, who were denied visas, sailed to China, since visas were not required to enter that country.

The remaining 150,000 Jews who would or could not leave were doomed to death. At the Wannsee Conference in 1942, the Nazis decreed that all Jews must face the "final solution" — the total annihilation of the Jewish people.

The Reichstag Is Burning!

At sixteen, Arthur Kahn was eyewitness to the terror instituted by the Nazis in 1933. He lived in Berlin with his father, a prosperous lawyer; his mother, and two younger brothers.

IN the fall of 1933 a knock sounded at our door. I opened it. Two SS men in black leather coats stood there.

"Herr Richard Kahn?"

"Just a minute," I said, staring at their black boots. "I will call him."

Father came into the hall. His face turned white. "Yes?"

"You are under arrest for crimes against the state," one of the men said. They seized him under the arms and dragged him towards the door.

"And what is my crime?" my father demanded.

"Sedition. We have been informed by the janitor that you have foreign books on your shelves."

"But I am a good German," Father said. "I served the Kaiser in World War I."

"You are making a mistake," cried Mother, who came into the hall as they were dragging him away.

When they shoved him into the elevator, Father called out, "Arthur, take care of your mother and brothers. Remember, you are the oldest." And he was gone.

Mother became hysterical. "Quick, Arthur, help me burn the French and English books." In a frenzy, she began to throw books into the woodburning stove in the kitchen.

"Mother," I protested, trying to stop her, "you're no better than the Nazis."

"What do you know, Arthur! You're only sixteen."

The next morning, Mother went to the police station to ask about Father. "You are wasting your time. Don't bother us," they told her.

I remembered February 27, the evening of the Reichstag fire, a few months earlier. The dark winter sky had turned

German passport of Hans and Fritz Kahn, Arthur's brothers.

red as our parliament building burned, and the flames illuminated the entire Tiergarten district. Wolf, Fritz and I stood at the window, watching in disbelief as the fire blazed unattended. We listened for the sirens and the fire trucks, but they never came. Mother refused to look out the window.

"Alyce," Father cried, seizing her by the shoulders and thrusting her in front of the curtain. "The Reichstag is burning. Can't you see it's time to leave."

Mother broke away. "It's only a temporary madness. Things will get better. My grandfather fought for Bismarck. It's only the foreign-born Jews who will have trouble."

"Alyce, a Jew is a Jew. We must leave — for the children's sake."

"I will not leave my parents and my homeland." My small, slim mother sat down in her damask chair and picked up her needlepoint. "You always said you were a German first and a Jew second."

We all stared at Mother. This was the first time she had ever defied Father. When he and his friends met on Saturdays to plan our emigration to South Africa earlier that year, she had not protested. Now our visas had arrived, but despite the fire below, she refused to leave.

"Fool," Father said to her, "Germany does not want me. I have accepted its decree."

The day after the Reichstag fire, all individual rights guaranteed by the Weimar Republic were suspended. Only Nazis could hold public meetings. All liberal newspapers were taken over by the Nazis. Truckloads of storm troopers in their brown uniforms roared down the Kaiser Alee and stopped before the apartment house next door. We watched from behind the curtains as several prominent writers and liberal thinkers were dragged out of the building.

Jewish businesses were boycotted, and my brothers and I were expelled from school. Signs were posted on park gates and theatres: "No Jews and Dogs Allowed."

Every week, Wolf, Fritz and I would stand at the apartment window and watch the Hitler Youth parade pass. How we wished the hated Hitler Youth, in their spotless uniforms, would tumble when they stopped to form a perfect pyramid!

One mild evening in May 1933, Wolf and I were returning from a meeting. As we strolled towards the University of Berlin, we noticed a crowd gathering in front of the Opernplatz. We stopped to see what was happening.

In single file, students marched out of the library, a lighted torch in one hand and books in the other. The flames cut an eerie red rim around the darkness. The students paused before a huge pile of burning books that had been collected by SS troops from other libraries.

As each student tossed his armload of books into the flames, an SS trooper called out over the loudspeaker the names of the "subversive authors" whose books were being destroyed: "Thomas Mann, Heinrich Heine, Albert Einstein,

Students gather to watch Nazis burn books that did not meet with Hitler's approval.

Erich Maria Remarque ..." Here and there, a protesting sheet, its edges singed, escaped the flames and floated across the Opernplatz.

After reading the list of the German authors, the SS trooper began to stumble through the names of condemned foreign writers: "Jack London, Upton Sinclair, Helen Keller ..."

Josef Goebbels, Minister of Propaganda, appeared to pronounce the final epitaph. The small, gnomish man stood before the students and spectators to say, "These flames not only illuminate the final end of an old era, they also light up a new one."

A month after my father's arrest, I was in the kitchen eating a sandwich of knockwurst and *ersatz* bread. I heard scratching at the window and looked up. Father stood on the fire escape dressed in a black and white prison uniform. He held his finger to his lips.

I opened the window, and he crawled inside, smelling of disinfectant.

"Are you all right?" I asked, as he embraced me. I looked at his gaunt face. His clothes hung on his slight frame. "Where were you?"

"Spandau prison. I pretended to have a heart attack, and they put me in the hospital. When the orderly went off the floor, I hid in the laundry truck and escaped." He wolfed down the remainder of my sandwich.

Mother heard our voices and came into the kitchen. "Richard," she said. "Thank God." Wolf and Fritz appeared.

"I've been watching the apartment house for hours," Father said. "The janitor just left for his Nazi party meeting. He must not know I've been here." Father took off the uniform. "Quickly, Arthur, pack some food while I change clothes. Fritz, burn this uniform."

While he changed, he rifled through the mail. There was a letter from Adolph Hitler. It read: "You have been awarded the Iron Cross for your service to the Kaiser during World War I." Father pocketed the letter and left.

A few hours after the Nazis discovered Father's escape, they came to our house. "Where is Richard Kahn?"

Mother stood there, trembling. "But you took him away. What have you done with him?" She was so petrified of the Nazis, her lying appeared believable.

"If he contacts you, you must inform us. Otherwise, there will be measures."

Mother fainted. When she came to, she said, "Arthur, you must join the Youth Aliyah. You must learn to become a farmer. Then you can go anywhere in the world. It's your only chance."

Youth Aliyah was a Zionist movement which trained young Jews to become farmers, so they could go to Palestine. The Nazis permitted this project because they wanted as many Jews as possible to leave the country. When I joined a nearby camp in Halbe, Fred Perlman, the director, taught me to milk cows and put me in charge of the barn. He also taught us Jewish songs and history, and pride in our Jewishness. After being subjected to Nazi propaganda telling us how inferior we were, we needed to develop self-esteem.

Meanwhile, the night my father left our house he had been hidden by his German employers. The next morning, he took a train to a town on the Czechoslovakian border. When he stepped onto the station platform, he saw a sign over the door: "Jews, enter this place at your own risk."

Father registered at a hotel a few blocks from the bridge leading to Czechoslovakia.

The police chief laughed at his request for a permit to visit an "insurance" client in Czechoslovakia. "No good German wants to leave Germany, sir. You are a traitor."

Im Namen des Führers und Reichskanzlers

Dem

Syndikus Dr. Richard K a h n

in Berlin — Wilmersdorf

ift auf Grund der Verordnung vom 13. Juli 1934 zur Erinnerung an den Weltkrieg 1914/1918 das von dem Reichspräsidenten Generalfeld= marschall von Hindenburg gestiftete

Ehrenkreuz für Kriegsteilnehmer

verliehen worden.

Berlin, den   1. März   193 5.

Der Polizeipräsident

J.A.

Nr. K. 196 /35.

Letter from Hitler awarding Dr. Richard Kahn a medal for service in World War I.

"A traitor? You are mistaken," Father replied, pulling out the letter from Hitler. "Would the Fuehrer award an Iron Cross to a traitor?"

"All right," the officer said, handing him a pass, "but leave your luggage in your hotel room."

Father walked over the bridge connecting the two countries. He had to figure out some way of retrieving his luggage.

At a small cafe overlooking the stream, he asked a waiter, "Can you go back and forth without a pass?"

"Of course. The guards know me."

"Here is the key to my room. Bring me my suitcase, and I shall share the contents with you." Father slipped him a large tip. The waiter promised to go at sunset.

At sunset, Father returned to the cafe and ordered a beer. As the accordion player struck up a polka, Father forced himself to sing and tap his feet in rhythm, just like the rest of the patrons.

Suddenly, there was a shot. The owner of the cafe rushed onto the terrace. "Someone sent my waiter for a suit-case, and it fell open, revealing hundreds of marks. The Ger-mans are holding the waiter."

All the patrons jumped up and ran towards the bridge. Father rose, but walked out the back door and thumbed a ride to Prague.

In Prague, a Jewish relief agency provided him with lodging, but before he went to sleep, Father sent a postcard to cousins in Charleston, West Virginia. It read: "I need help. Please contact me through the Joint Distribution Committee in Prague."

These distant cousins, now living in Baltimore, Mary-land, received the forwarded postcard. They immediately sent money and an affidavit, which promised the American gov-ernment that they would be responsible for Father when he emigrated to the United States. Father booked passage and arrived safely.

Once in Baltimore, Father grew more and more fran-tic. The German government refused to release us. He and his cousin approached the State Department in Washington, D.C. At first, the State Department said there was nothing they could do.

Father pleaded with the officials. "What kind of a government refuses to release a woman and three young boys because the father fled? They must get out of Germany. Each day the situation grows worse."

The State Department prodded the German Foreign Office. Because the 1936 Olympics were scheduled to take place in Berlin in only a few months, Germany wanted to appear reasonable to the rest of the world. Two years after Father's escape from prison, the Nazis granted us "valid for twenty-four hours only" passports. A slipsheet had been inserted with the passports: "Remember, you are a good German."

Father met us in New York. From the top of the Empire State Building, we gazed down on the skyscrapers and at Rockefeller Center, glowing with Christmas lights. In the morning, we took the train to Baltimore, filled with happiness for America and all things American. Here, life would be truly wonderful.

Father led us up the steps to our apartment on Spaulding Street. We stared at the mattresses supported by vegetable crates and at the kitchen table with its flaking blue paint. Our Baltimore cousins had stocked the kitchen, but aside from Father's books, which we had sent over the year before, the apartment was bare.

"We have a place to sleep and a place to eat," Mother said. She took out the only painting she had managed to save and hung it on the wall. "We are home. We will never talk about Germany again. As soon as we learn English, it will be the only language spoken in this house."

Arthur Kahn served with the United States Army during World War II. He is now an executive of a greeting card company. Once a year he returns to Germany to attend a convention. Each time his plane approaches the airport, he begins to perspire and to relive the deaths of his family and friends at the hands of the Nazis. "I tell myself over and over that it is time to forget . . . old prejudices should not be carried over to the next generation. But I still ask myself what I am doing on this plane."

The Night of Broken Glass

Manny Gale was fourteen years old on Crystal Night. His family's search for sanctuary led him to Cuba and then to the United States. Forty years later he told me of the terrifying details of that night.

I walked into the dining room of the Pentagon in 1959 to attend an important meeting with the Assistant Secretary of the Army, civilian experts and several generals. World War II had ended fourteen years ago and now Germany was being permitted to rearm.

The chief of staff came over and slapped me on the back. "Congratulations, Manny, you've been selected to help set up the German army."

Go back to Germany? He must be crazy. Let them get another armaments expert. I never wanted to see Germany again. "You've got the wrong guy," I said. "I don't want to go back."

My family had been among the lucky ones to get out of Germany in 1938, after Crystal Night.

My father and I were returning from a trip to Breslau. We had gone to visit my brothers at the Jewish boarding school there. I was shy and insecure at fourteen, and had chosen to put up with anti-Semitic taunts and beatings by my classmates in our local school. Even though Jews had been expelled from public schools, my parents had obtained special permission for me to remain.

As we approached our town of Trebnitz, my father and I stopped to look at the sunset. Instead, we saw smoke spiralling across the old fortress town.

"My God," Father cried. "Our house is on fire." He drove down the hill to the entrance of the town.

There was a barricade in front of the gate, and the mayor and chief of police, both in Nazi uniforms, stood on either side of the road block.

"What is the meaning of this?" my father demanded. "Remove it, immediately! My house is on fire."

"Not your house, not yet. It's your synagogue, Herr Gale. Get out; we are confiscating your car."

My father didn't move.

"Get out, Herr Gale, by order of the chief of police. Right now."

What was happening? Where were my mother and grandmother and grandfather?

"We wish you luck," the mayor shouted as he started our car, "if you live through the night. Heil Hitler."

"If we live through the night, Dad?" What did they mean? For the first time since I was a small boy, he took my hand. I wanted to run, but couldn't. A terrible fear grew in me.

I forced one foot to go in front of the other. I had begged my parents to leave Germany a year ago. It was after I had been humiliated for the hundredth time. Someone had slipped a watch into my pocket and then accused me of stealing.

"At least, send me to Palestine with the Youth Aliyah," I had pleaded. My father had lectured me about keeping our family together.

The street was silent. Usually, there were ambulances racing past the hospital and people coming from Mass at St. Hedwig's Church. My father's hand held mine tighter.

A sheet with a crude drawing of a Jew, his head severed, floated across Goldstein's barber shop. Father stumbled on some broken glass. I saw a sign above the shoemaker's door: "Let the Jew croak."

We turned the corner. Noise exploded in our ears as a revolving spotlight on the back of a truck flashed from one end of the street to another. Storm troopers stood on the truck shouting directions to the townspeople through a bull-horn: "Destroy everything Jewish. Let nothing remain." The spotlight swung to our store. An effigy of Father with a noose around his neck hung from a second story window. The crowd threw itself against the windows.

My father and I tried to push our way through the crowd, but four SS troopers grabbed him by the arms. They pushed him to his knees and made him crawl towards the synagogue.

I slipped into a drugstore. "A tube of toothpaste," I mumbled, wondering if I could sneak out the back.

"Get out; you can't hide here."

I opened the door of the pharmacy. My classmates were waiting for me outside. My chemistry partner, Gunter, seized my right arm and took the toothpaste from my hand. Two boys held me while he smeared it on my face. Someone else ripped my trouser leg with a broken beer bottle. I kicked and thrashed as my neighbor Ulrich ripped off my shirt.

"To the fire, to the fire," the bullhorn urged. The spotlight flashed on the burning synagogue. The mob ran towards the blaze.

I raced home. "Mother, Grandmother, where are you?"

"Upstairs. We're on the second floor. Manny, run away. They took Grandfather, and they'll take you. Hide." My mother trembled as she and my grandmother huddled on the upstairs landing, behind two upholstered chairs.

The spotlight focused on our house. A huge log shattered the oak doors. Hundreds of people surged inside, yelling, screaming, laughing, knocking over the furniture, pulling up the rugs and stripping the closets. I stood there, shocked, furious, helpless.

"Look out the windows, Jews," the bullhorn blared. "Look at your synagogue burning. Citizens, return to the square."

A synagogue in flames, Crystal Night, 1938.

Obediently, the mob turned and walked away.

From our window, we could see my father and grandfather and eight other Jewish men chained together, forced to dance around the synagogue. The town band struck up a Strauss waltz as the stained glass windows crashed to the ground.

I could not stand it any longer. I ran downstairs and through the crowds to shield my grandfather.

"Swine," a storm trooper shouted. He chained me between Father and Grandfather. The heat of the burning synagogue singed my body. How long could Grandfather last?

"Stop," the voice over the bullhorn directed. "Unchain the Jews. The fire is spreading."

The storm troopers removed the chains and handcuffed the men in groups of twos and threes. I was overlooked. When a burning beam fell across the square, the crowd retreated. In the confusion, I ran home. Grandmother and Mother were still cowering behind the chairs.

Through the open window I could hear the bullhorn re-directing the mob to our house: "The synagogue is finished. Back to the Gale house. Heil Hitler."

"Come on. We've got to get out of here," I said. But before we could leave, the crowd came, with unbelievable

fury, armed with rifles, sticks, pipes, crowbars. They tore the tiles off the ovens, overturned the china closets, and ripped the ivories off the piano keys. Even the heavy oak furniture, that four servants hadn't been able to move when we had redecorated, was splintered into fragments. Only the maids' rooms were saved. The two servants had locked themselves in their rooms.

"It's our quarters, not the Jew's," they told the storm trooper. "Don't you touch it."

"Leave them alone," the storm trooper said. "It's cold outside." He lifted his bullhorn. "Germans, there are Jews in this house. Do your duty."

Storm troopers rounding up Jews on Crystal Night.

A hundred contorted faces rushed up the stairs and swirled into one monstrous gargoyle. I fought to stay conscious, but collapsed.

When I woke up, a storm trooper was standing over me. "Get out of the house, Jews, and don't come back. And if I find a gun in this house, you'll all be shot before the day is out." He walked out of the house.

I led my mother and grandmother out into the street. For the first time in my fourteen years I was in charge.

A woman whose son and husband had been seized by the Nazis sheltered us that night in her apartment. She was half-crazed with grief. At six in the morning, storm troopers knocked at her door.

"All of you, out. No Jews allowed in this building."

I could only lead Mother and Grandmother home. There was nowhere else to go. On the way, a stooped, white-haired tramp bumped into me. His face was distorted by purple and red welts. He could barely focus his sunken eyes.

"Excuse us," I muttered and steered the women from his path. Gentile shopkeepers, sweeping the glass from the pavement, looked the other way as we passed. The stinging odor of last night's fire clung to the walls of the town despite the crisp November air.

Our house was a shambles, except for the maids' rooms. Grandmother collapsed on one of the beds.

There was a knock at the door. A neighbor stood there supporting the white-haired tramp we had bumped into earlier. "This is your grandfather. He has been wandering up and down our street, unable to recognize the house he has lived in for forty years."

I sank to the floor. I remembered the answer we had gotten from our American cousins in response to my parents' request for my brothers and I to "visit" them.

*One of many store windows
shattered on Crystal Night.*

"You are exaggerating your situation," they had written. "No civilized nation could possibly permit such intolerance. Things will straighten out."

There was a tap at the window. I looked up at the broad face of Johann, a farmer who had been in the army with Father in World War I. He knocked aside the shards of glass and passed eggs, butter, cheese, bread, and winter apples through the window.

23

A few days later, when Grandfather had recovered, we went to the bank. Grandfather was one of the directors.

The clerk, who had always fawned over him, was curt. "Your funds have been confiscated by the Third Reich to pay for the damages caused by you Jews on Crystal Night."

For six weeks we worried about Father. Then a letter arrived from Buchenwald, the camp where my father had been imprisoned: "Please send me the certificate awarding me the Iron Cross. The authorities are releasing those who were decorated in World War I."

In March, we received another notice. "Herr Gale will be released providing he leaves the country within six weeks. If he is still in Germany after that time, he will be reinterned."

Six weeks! Grandfather went to a contact. "Bankrupt me, but get me seven visas. No, five visas. My wife and I are too old. Our fate is in Germany."

Every day I went to the station to look for Father. One day, three cripples, supporting one another, hobbled slowly down the steps of the train. I didn't recognize any of their battered faces.

"Manny, Manny, it's Dad," one of them called. He limped towards me, filthy and unshaven, his elbow protruding from his skin.

"How did you break your arm and nose?" I whispered.

"To get into Buchenwald we had to jump down seventy feet, over dead bodies. Enough. Of some things, we shouldn't talk."

The next day we left for Hamburg, where we would board a ship. We sat in our small cabin, not quite believing our good fortune, as our ship (jammed to double capacity) steamed free of Germany.

Two days out of Portugal, the captain called Father to his cabin and handed him a telegram.

Father's hand trembled as he read it. "It has come to light that Herr Gale participated in underground activities against the Third Reich. You are to turn the ship around and return the entire family to Hamburg."

"I don't know what this is all about," said Father, his face ashen. "I served the Kaiser in World War I. I still have a hole at the bottom of my spine and scars."

The captain took out his cigarette lighter. "I have the authority to arrest you, but if I did not receive the message, I cannot act." The paper turned to ashes.

When we entered the Havana harbor, a boat pulled up alongside the ship. A rotund gentleman in a khaki uniform climbed aboard. Everyone lined up to present their visas. We were first. Father opened his briefcase and pulled out the papers.

"These are no good," the official said. "The entrance price has been raised. You must provide an additional three hundred dollars per person."

Father stared at the man. "Fifteen hundred dollars? But we were only permitted to take fifty dollars."

"Then you'll have to return to Germany." He nodded to the captain. "Take them back."

Mother screamed. "Look at his arm. Look at his broken nose. We'll be killed."

"Sh!" my father said. He turned to the customs officer. "I have relatives in the United States. They will send the money."

"You will have to wait in prison."

Through the barred windows of Triste Cunha, an island in the harbor, we watched the tiny filaments of foam break against the shore.

"Cheer up," Father said. "This isn't Buchenwald. Admire the coconut palms; taste the fresh pineapple the jailer brought us."

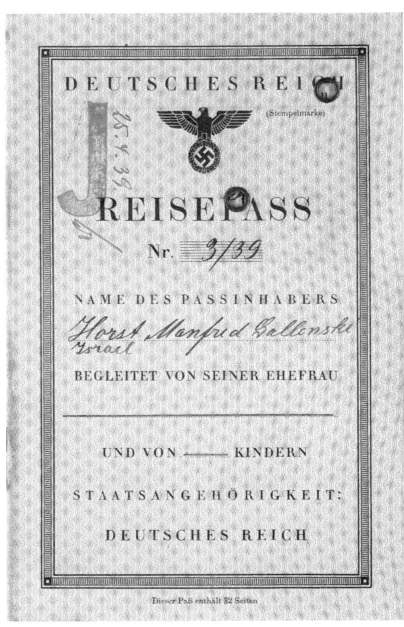

Passports issued to Jews at that time were all stamped with a J.

Manny Gale's German passport.

"After Germany, jail looks pretty good," my brother Richard said, stepping on the largest cockroach I had ever seen. "But it doesn't hold much of a future."

Father started to hum, always a good sign. "If the big shots take bribes, then the little fish do, too." He offered our jailer the entire fifty dollars we had been permitted to bring out of Germany. Within an hour we sailed past the island in a motor launch into Havana, like a family on a picnic. Father found a hotel that served three meals a day, and Richard and I stuffed ourselves with papayas and mangoes. The last few months had forced us to lose our baby fat.

My family thought it best to leave Cuba as quickly as we could. To learn American ways, I joined a camp for refugee boys run by American Quakers outside Havana. There, in the lush green hills of Cuba, this friendless, tormented, rich boy learned to build houses, cut sugar cane, and harvest fruit. It was one of the most formative experiences in my life. When our visas for America came, I packed my bag and looked forward to a new life.

Two years after Crystal Night, our relatives welcomed us as we stepped off the train in Richmond, Virginia.

In 1943, just before my eighteenth birthday, I enlisted in the American Air Corps. In six months I would be dropping bombs on Germany. One day, my commanding officer called me into his office. "You can't become a pilot. You're an enemy alien. We're sending you to the Army medical school."

"Medical school? Colonel, I don't plan to spend six years fighting the war with a microscope. I refuse to go."

"How can a Jew boy refuse to go to medical school?"

I insisted.

"You'll be sorry. I'm transferring you to the 100th Infantry Division."

As part of the 100th Infantry Division Intelligence Staff, I became an expert in sabotage and prisoner interrogation. On one of my first missions, I put on a German uniform and slipped across the border from France into Germany. We planned to release American and Russian prisoners of war who were being held in a nearby German camp. Marie, our guide, was a French resistance leader. She led us through a cave to a narrow valley. Below, German guards marched back and forth in front of the camp.

I approached the gate. "Heil Hitler. I was separated from my division. Can the commandant give me food and transportation back to my unit?"

As the sentries took me to the commanding officer, the men from my patrol slipped inside the now unguarded compound, released the Russian and American prisoners and took over the camp. I divided the prisoners we had freed into groups, giving each of my men the responsibility for escorting the ex-prisoners through the German lines to safety. Since I was in German uniform, I headed back to our lines alone.

The American soldier at our base looked beautiful, even with his gun pointed at me.

"Manny Gale, Corporal, 100th Infantry," I said, forgetting that I was still wearing a German uniform.

"Who won the World Series of 1943?" he demanded, his machine gun only inches from my chest.

"This is 1945."

"Don't try to fake it, Kraut. Give the right answer — live. Give the wrong answer, well, I ain't got no time for takin' prisoners."

"Take me to the C.O. I'm in counter-intelligence, 100th Infantry. The C.O. will verify my status."

"What's the password for today?"

"For God's sake," I said, "I was out all night on a

mission. Do you want me to sing 'Dixie' before you take me to the C.O.?"

"That might not be a bad idea. Sing, Kraut, sing."

I sang "Dixie," off-key, in my heavily-accented English, loud and clear.

I was lucky on that mission. But just a few days before the war ended, I was wounded by a German rocket. It took thirteen operations in thirteen months, but the doctors saved my arm.

Manny Gale was awarded the Exceptional Civilian Service Award three times by the American government. He recently retired from government service and is now employed by private industry. He lives in Virginia with his wife and three children.

AUSTRIA

To the Jew who had settled in Austria before the Middle Ages, Austria became known as "Eretz ha Damin," the Bloodstained Land. The Jewish community in Austria was subjected to frequent massacres and often faced extinction. To justify mass killings of Jews, the charge of Blood Libel (stealing a Christian child, fattening him up and slaughtering him for use in the Passover ritual) was used, even though the Hebrew Bible specifically forbids blood sacrifices. Jews were also accused of desecrating the Host, the thin bread-like wafer used in the Catholic service to represent the body of Christ. Jews were supposedly guilty of stealing the Host and harming it to cause Christ pain.

In addition to the frequent threats on their lives, Jews were subject to forced conversion to Christianity or expulsion from the country. Jewish families who were of service to the royal family, or rich enough to offer bribes, were permitted to remain in Vienna. In an effort to hold down the growth of the Jewish community, a law was passed in 1727 permitting only the oldest son of a Jewish family to marry and have children.

By the nineteenth century, however, many Jewish families prospered as bankers and industrialists. In the early twentieth century, Jews were granted the rights of citizenship and were active in the arts, sciences, and businesses. Intermarriage became common.

Despite the proximity of Hitler and the growing strength of German military forces, few Austrian Jews felt threatened enough to flee. This changed the day the Germans marched into Austria, March 12, 1938. The Austrians welcomed the Nazis with cheers and bouquets of flowers. The invasion became known as the Blumenkriege, the Flower War.

Before the end of 1939 126,000 Jews escaped Austria. Those who were forced to remain were deported to concentration camps. A remnant survived.

In 1970, there were 12,000 Jews living in Austria. In that year, Bruno Kreisky, of Jewish parentage, became chancellor of Austria, and as of 1982, he continues to hold that position.

Beneath the Mountains

Erich was fifteen when the Nazis marched into Austria on March 12, 1938. Within a few months, he was in exile and entirely on his own.

Herr Kroner stood at the door. I was frightened. This was the first time I had seen him in Nazi uniform. Still, I had to admire the crispness of his uniform and the shine on his boots.

His arm shot forward. "Heil Hitler," he shouted. Then he began to whisper. "I have come to repay your father's kindness in not revealing to the Austrian authorities that I was a member of the Nazi party." He looked up and down the hall. "Erich, you must leave at once. The S.S. is coming to arrest you."

"Me? I'm a student. Why?"

"You are accused of posting obscene literature." Nervously, he rubbed the beginning of a blonde mustache.

Obscene literature? My head was full of Latin poets, Virgil and Homer. I had no time for sexual fantasies. I dreamed of becoming a professor.

"Yes, obscene literature. The posters you put up advertising the Austrian elections." Herr Kroner looked up and down and vanished.

Where could I go? All day long I had been glued to the radio, a fear growing within me as I listened to Chancellor Schuschnigg's resignation. I was shocked by the wild rantings that followed with Hitler proclaiming, "One people, one empire, one leader." My mother was in Czechoslovakia visiting her parents. My father was in his dry goods store. I had to disappear and leave my father alone in the middle of a crisis.

I walked down the steps and outside. Instantaneous Nazism! The swastika billowed over the Staatsopera, the Town Hall, the Imperial Palace. The cobbler's shop, the stationers, even the sacher torte in Demel's bakery window flaunted a Nazi flag. Suddenly Vienna, the city with the best cinnamon buns, the best water, the city with a golden heart, had turned into an evil witch. As I stood there, not knowing where to go, I saw two German soldiers stop an elderly Jew.

"Swine," the young soldier shouted. He twisted the old man's hands behind his back while the other soldier set fire to his beard.

My fellow Austrians stood there, laughing. I apologized to myself. This cannot represent all Austrians. Some groups will rise up to fight Hitler. Even as I tried to reassure myself, I looked up and saw storm troopers pushing Jews out of high windows.

I wandered around until nightfall. Then I knocked at the door of my father's former bookkeeper.

He hid me and called my father. Through a Christian friend, father contacted my mother's family in Czechoslovakia. They sent us a message. "Be at the Czech border at midnight."

That evening, my father and I hid in the woods and waited. At midnight, we saw Uncle Chaim approach the Czech guards. He handed them some money. The guards turned their backs. We crossed over.

"You have to maintain a low profile," Uncle Chaim said, as he drove us to a farmhouse. "The Hlinka, the Czech Fascists, are searching for refugees. I've found both of you night jobs. You'll be safe for a few days."

Every night, father unlocked the door of a factory and worked as an accountant. At 3 o'clock each morning, I pulled a cap over my forehead and delivered milk. As the horses hooves clattered across the empty cobblestone streets, I wondered over and over how my countrymen could let this happen.

Every few nights, we moved to avoid the Czech Fascists. In late September, I came home from my milk run to find the Hlinka waiting. With several hundred other refugees, we were driven like cattle towards the Hungarian border.

In Dunaskstralia, Hungary, the Hlinka disappeared.

I shivered in the chill September air and looked for sticks to start a fire. There were none. Young and old, we huddled together. At dawn, the local farmers bringing their potatoes and apples to market took pity on us. They brought us poles and canvas and helped us to set up tents.

35

A few days later, Hungarian troops marched into Dunaskstralia. "Who are these people?" the captain asked.

"Refugees. The Czechs drove them here," the mayor responded.

"They can't stay. Swine, pick up your belongings." The captain stopped a train and ordered us to board. After a short ride, we were forced at whip's length to march until we came to a farmhouse. When the captain shouted, "Halt," everyone tried to get inside the narrow shelter. I collapsed on the ground and fell asleep.

In the morning, the captain lined us up. "I want all your valuables. Anyone withholding jewels or money will be shot."

I stood there, angry, not moving. The few kroner in my rucksack were mine.

My mother whispered, "Erich, you must."

Reluctantly, I handed over my last coins.

Satisfied, the captain herded us along a flat road just behind the Hungarian border. It was an unclaimed strip of land, one kilometer long sandwiched between Slovakia and Hungary.

"Stop," the captain shouted.

Our group had swollen to over five hundred people. It included pregnant women, children, old men, adolescents, families and now, the dead. We elected leaders and again scoured the ground for wood to build shelters. Here, too, every stick had been scavenged.

I thought about running into the woods. No, I couldn't leave my parents. That night, some of the boys did slip away. We heard shots and screams.

In the morning, a Hungarian colonel drove up in a jeep. A bedraggled family that he had discovered squatting on the banks of the Danube sat beside him. He stared at us and wept.

We wept with him.

After several minutes, he composed himself. "What in God's name, can I do for you?"

Our spokesman stood up. "We have not eaten in two days. We would like food, medicine and shelter. We also request permission to send the sick, the pregnant and the dead to Bratislava."

An hour later, the colonel returned. "You may send your dead to Bratislava. Everyone else must remain here. The Jewish community of Bratislava will be permitted to bring you food and tents."

Delivery trucks and private cars loaded with food and tents drove into "no-man's land." As soon as the tents were up, a slow drizzle began to fall. Without floors, the stakes and canvas melted into the mud.

"It's hopeless," my uncle said. He went to the Jewish community in Bratislava. "Please give me permission to rescue my sister and her family."

That evening, Uncle Chaim returned to "no-man's land" with a car filled with huge sacks of bread and salami. When the sacks were empty, we crawled inside and were lifted into the trunk of the car. He drove us directly to the railroad station.

By the time the train reached Prague, our detention in "no-man's land" had been publicized in the French and Swedish papers. While many countries criticized the Hungarians, none of them offered to take the refugees. The Bolivian consul did permit the Joint Distribution Commit-tee, a Jewish refugee organization, to buy visas to Bolivia. Within a few days, we were on a boat to South America.

When the boat docked at Arica, Chile, I was overwhelmed by the stench of excrement and rotten fish that was carried past the wharves by the Humboldt current. A constant film of fine dust blew over the windswept city. The snow-
-covered Andes stood at a distance, foreboding guardians of an incredibly blue sky.

My parents and I followed the flow of donkeys, sheep and vendors to the town square. People squatted on the ground, surrounded by fruits, flowers, wandering chickens and clay pots. This was a new world: bleak, primitive, a world lacking in European culture.

The train to La Paz, Bolivia, struggled across the Andes, passing slag heaps and llamas loaded with sacks of ore. Closer to the city, more and more people, some riding burros or driving goats and sheep to the market, crowded the dirt roads. La Paz lay in a ravine on the Choquepyapu River. Corrugated tin roofs capped the adobe huts clinging to the sides of the steep streets that bordered the gorge.

The first morning, I awakened with a terrible headache. I walked out of the hotel to the plaza. A man with a loudspeaker was shouting, "The Jews are the scum of the earth."

I had not really escaped.

I knew I couldn't be a financial burden to my parents. I took the only only work I could find. From a temperature of 20 degrees, at an altitude of twelve thousand feet, I descended barefoot into the tin mines. The lower I climbed, the warmer the air became. By the time I reached my workplace, I was stripped to my waist. The heat became so intense, I had to constantly stop and pour water over my body to prevent dehydration. At the end of the day, I ascended to the shock of cold air at the top of the mine. Like my Indian co-workers, I slept in a thatched windowless hut and subsisted on a diet of meal and rice. But whenever I heard that someone had just arrived from Europe, I put on my European suit and went to meet them.

"Did you bring any books?" I asked once I introduced myself. "And may I borrow them?"

Whenever I could, I lay on my mattress and read German, Spanish, French or English. My introduction to English came through LIFE magazine. I asked the American mining engineers to read the stories to me. I would memorize the words and match them with the print. I lived with the hope that the war would be over and I could soon return to Austria and my studies.

On June 14, 1940, the day Paris fell, the entire refugee colony poured out into the square and wept. As the war continued to go badly for the Allies in 1941 and 1942, I lost hope. By 1942, I was so overworked and exhausted that I became physically and mentally ill. I knew I had to escape the soul–and body–robbing climate of Bolivia. I said good bye to my parents and fled to Santiago, Chile. In this European-like city with its broad streets and beautiful parks, I felt less stifled. I peddled bananas, taught French and German, worked as a carpenter and as a farm hand. Occasionally, I had enough money for a movie or a concert. Still, I felt empty and incomplete. I went to Equador where I had European friends.

The subhuman conditions in the mines had weakened my body. For weeks, I was delirious with typhoid fever and dysentery. My friends took care of me until I could work. Though not completely cured, I found a job as an accountant with the United Fruit Company. For the first time I could save money. I was determined to get rid of these recurring illnesses.

In 1948, ten years after I left Austria, I applied for a humanitarian visa to the United States. A Jewish welfare organization in New York gave me eighteen dollars a week for room and board. I became an outpatient at Mt. Sinai hospital in New York City.

The doctors found 28 different parasites in my gastrointestinal tract and over a period of months treated me until I was cured. In my free time I discovered the New York Public Library. I also contacted a former classmate from Vienna who was now a student at Harvard. He invited me to visit.

In self-soled shoes and in the same Charlie Chaplinesque suit that I had worn from Prague to South America, I toured the Harvard Yard and attended classes. A yearning to be a part of the intellectual world seized me.

When I returned to Quito, I enrolled in the university. It offered no challenge. Every day, I mailed three letters of application to colleges all over the world. Out of the hundreds of letters I sent, only one college replied. A small Catholic school in Ohio offered me a position as a language instructor. A check for the boat fare was included. It was from a non-Jewish refugee physicist who had also fled from Vienna. He wrote, "You are to make no attempt to repay this loan until you are better off than I am."

My dream of becoming a professor was about to come true.

Erich received his B.A. and M.A. in two years. Following the award of his doctorate, he obtained a Guggenheim Fellowship. A Fullbright lectureship followed. Today, he holds a chair at one of America's most distinguished universities.

CZECHOSLOVAKIA

In Prague, the capital of Czechoslovakia, stands one of the oldest remaining synagogues in Europe, the Alte-Neue Schul. This thirteenth century building is evidence of a Jewish community that dates back to Roman times.

It was not until the creation of the Republic of Czechoslovakia in 1918 that Jews attained rights of citizenship and the country became known as a "paradise" among Jews. The universities were open to all, and many foreign-born Jews, prevented by restrictive quotas from entering universities at home, were able to obtain degrees from these schools.

In 1938, Hitler threatened to seize the Czechoslovakian Sudetenland region by force. He claimed it belonged to

Germany. Great Britain, France, and Italy, with the hope of preventing another war and of "buying peace in our time," forced Czechoslovakia to hand it over to Hitler. Eight hundred thousand citizens and one-fifth of the country were exchanged for Hitler's promise of "no further territorial ambitions."

On March 15, 1939, German troops invaded the rest of the country. The Jews of Bratislavia, Czechoslovakia, were among the first to be deported to the concentration camps in 1941. Despite appeals by Jewish leaders and a protest by the Vatican, additional deportations to the Auschwitz death camp followed, decimating the Jewish population.

The once-thriving Jewish community in Czechoslovakia has been reduced to a historical footnote. The Alte-Neue Schul is also a Jewish museum. Ironically, its collection of rare scrolls and religious objects had been established by the Germans to serve as "The Central Museum of the Defunct Jewish Race," a prophecy which has nearly been fulfilled for the Jews of Czechoslovakia.

The Jungle

Lisa Liebschutz Rozsa left Czechoslovakia at eighteen. Her search for freedom
led from her homeland to Iraq to Palestine to Uganda to Kenya.

I clutched the Iraqi entry permit and hurried to Gestapo headquarters. In the short month since the German invasion of Czechoslovakia on March 15, 1939, my whole world had changed. Even the traffic was topsy-turvy. Germans had torn down the street signs and replaced them with German names. Huge *swastikas* hung like dirty linen over the buildings.

My father's business had been taken away and given to his assistant. Now, at eighteen, I had a ticket to freedom. It had been sent by my fiance, Imre Rozsa. I had met Imre when he was a student at the university. When he graduated, the only position he could find was in Iraq, a British protectorate, in the Arabian desert. If the Gestapo would allow me to leave, I could join him.

Citizens weep as they watch the Nazis' triumphant parade into Czechoslovakia in 1939.

I trembled as I waited inside the headquarters. From every door the shrieks and pleas of the tortured cried out. I dug my fingers into the underside of my chair until my nails split. Then I heard my name called.

I faced the German officer. He was very young, immaculately dressed. "Are you a Zionist?"

"No."

"Are you a Communist?" he stared at me. "Do you owe any water or electric bills?"

"No." This was ridiculous.

He stamped a paper and handed it to me. "You are free to leave."

It was April 18, 1939. I ran home and packed. I didn't cry. The tears of farewell for my family and country remained suspended.

In Prague, I went to the British Consulate, where my Iraqi permit allowed me to go to the head of the line of five thousand imploring Jews. From there, I went to Cook's Travel Agency to pick up my ticket. As I put it in my handbag, I heard a voice say, "I want the identical passage you sold to the Jewess, Lisa Liebschutz."

I turned to stare at the short, stocky woman behind me. "We shall be companions," she said. With a stiff-legged step, she picked up my suitcase and led me out of the office. I realized I couldn't get rid of her. There were Nazi soldiers on every corner. I followed her silently to the train station.

Throughout the ride from Austria to the Italian port of Genoa, she shouted questions at me. "Did you ever attend Zionist meetings? Tell me, did your parents send money to Palestine? What are the names of your underground colleagues? Where is the money your parents have in hiding?"

I turned my head toward the window and searched the forest for the first violets of spring. If only I could remain silent, perhaps she would stop. The view of the ships in Genoa harbor made me feel better. I stood up to reach for my bag.

"No," she pushed my hand away. "I am your cabin mate. I will take it."

On board ship, I lay on the bed, afraid to go to sleep. Finally, I dozed, exhausted by the strain of the past eighteen hours. A short while later I was jolted awake.

The woman was leaning over me. "Whore, tell me, did you ever attend Zionist meetings? Whore, speak."

I pushed her away and went out onto the deck. As the sun rose over Alexandria, Egypt, a British cruiser steamed into the harbor. The sight of the British flag reassured me.

When I walked into the dining room a cablegram lay at my plate. "All our love and best wishes to you and Imre on your marriage. Mother and Dad."

The tears exploded. I sat there, aware of everyone staring at me, unable to stop crying.

When we docked in Beirut, Lebanon, my Gestapo shadow left me. I removed my heavy jacket and sank down on my suitcase, overpowered by the heat and stench. Barefoot children surrounded me; the odor of urine was everywhere.

I watched the Arab women, their black veils covering everything but their eyes, balancing water jugs on their heads. Western women in knee-length dresses brushed past them. Men wearing fezzes, turbans, helmets, and Panama hats paused under the colorful canopies of the marketplace.

At the bus depot I boarded the Trans-Desert bus for the two-day trip to Damascus, Syria. The golden monotony of sand, rocks, and dunes dazzled my eyes. From Damascus the travel agency had arranged for a taxi to take me across the roadless desert to Baghdad.

Imre was waiting there for me. In an ancient synagogue in Iraq, Imre and I stood beneath a marriage canopy and repeated our vows in Hebrew.

Iraq offered a young architect like Imre fantastic

opportunities. He designed palaces and harems, a department store. After the terror of Czechoslovakia, this strange, Oriental world held work, security, and friends.

A few months after my arrival, that security vanished. When his employees returned to India, Imre obtained a job with the Ministry of Defense. Then, Rashid Ali, an Iraqi who had spent many years in Germany, was appointed prime minister. Jews had to go into hiding.

Rashid Ali approached Sir Winston Churchill, offering to help the Allies if they would give him Palestine. Churchill refused to make a deal. Ali turned to Hitler. He willingly gave Ali arms, money and the promise of the Holy Land.

Hitler had a grand plan to win the war in the spring of 1941. Part of the plan included Rashid Ali, who was to overthrow the royal family and force the surrender of British troops stationed in Iraq. A successful coup in Iraq would have helped to cut off the British access to oil and to the sea.

Rashid Ali surrounded the British air base of Habbaniya, just outside Basra. He ordered the British to surrender. While the Iraqis waited for an answer, night fell and they went to sleep. At dawn, a white flag was flying over the fort. With battle cries, the Iraqis stormed the gates. One by one, the British gunned them down. The Iraqis fled just before the British ammunition gave out.

Now that British protection had been restored, it was safe for Jews to come out of hiding. Imre was walking down the street when a British soldier stopped him and demanded his passport. Imre handed it to him.

The soldier looked at it. "You dirty Nazi, up against the wall." He motioned Imre back into the dark alley.

"That's a Hungarian passport, not a German one," Imre protested.

"A Nazi is a Nazi. Over to the wall." He cocked his rifle.

"No," Imre edged out onto the sunny boulevard.

"Murder me in the middle of the avenue. I ran away from the Nazis. If you are a decent chap, you'll take me to Captain Tole and let him decide."

Captain Tole vouched for Imre, and he was hired as a civilian supervisor of public works with the Tenth Indian Army. We packed our belongings and crossed the desert to Basra where Imre would help construct hospitals and runways.

The civility of the British government did not last. The war was going badly for the Allies. All enemy aliens — Jews as well as Nazis — were rounded up and put on trains. No one would tell us where we were going.

I stared out the window at the desert. I had been on a continuous journey since I left Czechoslovakia to come to Iraq.

Our train stopped in Palestine. I clung to Imre as the British ordered the men separated from the women. Would I see him again?

The soldiers took the women to a convent outside Jerusalem. Every day, I begged for news of the men. But the nuns just smiled and continued their devotions, kindly white figures sheltered by the crucifix, untouched by a flaming world.

Two months later the men returned in open trucks, and we were all taken to another train. As we approached the Suez Canal, fighter planes swept back and forth across the desert. The train stopped; the passengers flung themselves onto the ground. I saw a ship explode in the harbor, flinging its crew across the water. Two hundred yards away a plane crashed, its flaming parts falling across the desert.

After the battle, the British put us aboard a converted Italian troop ship, the *Esperia*. We docked at Mombassa, Kenya, in East Africa. There we gazed at the lovely beach and thought we had surely reached paradise. Europeans rushed to greet us, bringing food and clothing.

Our joy lasted only a few hours. We were soon herded onto another train, but this time we passed through the jungle. A hundred miles into the bowels of the earth, the train stopped at Camp Makindu. Walls of jungle growth pushed against the small barbed wire clearing. Two hundred army cots, placed side by side, filled a dirt-floored tent. Our food was heated in big pots over a pile of rocks. There was barely enough water to drink. There were other dangers, too; Imre smashed a cobra that had slithered into the hole they were digging for latrines.

The Nazis among us marched around the cot of a woman dying of blackwater fever singing "Deutschland Uber Alles" (Germany Over All), to prove their superiority.

Those of us who spoke English wrote to the Nairobi Hebrew Congregation. "In the name of God and our ancient ties, we beseech you to help us. Conditions here are inhumane. If we are not taken from this camp, we will die."

The delegation from Nairobi arrived in spotless white suits. They gazed at our filthy bodies and emaciated figures and fled with promises to obtain our release. We never heard from them again.

A week later the Red Cross condemned our camp as "unfit for human habitation," and the British took us by train to Lake Victoria, Entebbe. The lake was full of fish and lush tropical fruits surrounded us.

With clean bodies and contented stomachs, Imre and I sat on our cots and looked at each other. There were no books, pencils, paper, or work.

"I can stand it no longer," Imre said after erasing a map of our journey which he had drawn in the dirt. "I'm going to volunteer to work for the Ministry of Roads."

Imre's new job instantly provided us with a house, two servants, a stove, a filled refrigerator, and fine silver. Though we were comfortable, we were still formally prisoners. Imre went to the Chief Secretary of Uganda and asked him how we could be freed.

"Join the British Army," he told him.

I protested. "You'll be sent away. I have no one but you."

"Lisa," Imre said, "I shall not be able to face our children after the war when they ask, 'What did you do in the fight against Hitler?' and I have to reply, 'I sat in an internment camp and let other men fight my battles.' "

Fortunately, Imre was sent to Nairobi and I could go with him. While he worked as an engineer, I worked as a secretary to the British Army. One morning I received a letter from the British Commissioner: "As an enemy alien, you are to report for immediate repatriation."

Imre had been sent to Mombassa for a week. I was alone. I hailed a rickshaw and rode to headquarters. "My husband is a British officer. You cannot do this to me."

The doctor ignored me. "Line up for your shots. We'll wait until your husband comes home."

I didn't know where to turn. I sent a message to the Chief Secretary of Uganda. He telephoned me immediately. "Apply for formal release, and I will recommend it."

For hours, I wrote and rewrote the letter, anxious to use the right phrases. A few days later, my request was approved. I was permitted to remain in Kenya with Imre.

After the war, the Rozsas elected to stay in Nairobi. "Europe is full of death, and Kenya is full of opportunity," they said. Imre is now one of the country's leading architects, and Lisa is an insurance broker. Their three children were raised in Kenya. Lisa's mother, who survived Auschwitz, joined them there.

The Nairobi Hebrew Congregation designed by Imre Rosza.

POLAND

The Nazi extermination of three million Polish Jews ended a one-thousand-year-old history. Despite extended periods of persecution by Polish rulers and church leaders, Jewish cultural and religious institutions had flourished. Rabbinical schools, or *yeshivas,* had supplied rabbis to Jewish communities throughout the world. Jews in other countries found inspiration and enrichment from the theater, music, poetry and literature produced by Polish Jews.

     The Jews had first come to Poland from the Middle East centuries before the birth of Christ. Jews from Germany and Czechoslovakia, fleeing the Crusaders, followed in the eleventh and twelfth centuries.

In the thirteenth century, the Polish king, Boleslav, invited Jewish merchants from Germany to come to Poland and offered them the protection of the Crown. They brought with them the Yiddish language, a mixture of Hebrew and German.

Medieval Poland was a vast country comprising what is now the Ukraine, White Russia, Lithuania, and Poland. Since the nobles lacked the desire to oversee their remote estates, they hired Jews to manage them and market the produce. Jews, who had been persecuted in the cities, flocked to these underdeveloped areas. Shtetls, or communities of Jews, grew up around these estates.

The Jews, who could read and write, were appointed tax collectors, customs inspectors, and overseers. This did not add to their popularity with the peasants. Between 1648 and 1649, Chmielnicki, the Cossack peasant leader, and his troops swept across the country destroying shtetls and slaughtering over one hundred thousand Jews.

In the eighteenth century two movements arose that affected Jews throughout Eastern Europe. For the masses, too poor to devote their days to prayer and study, the teachings of the Baal Shem Tov (Master of the Good Name) — through song, dance, and righteous living one could attain the highest spirituality — offered fulfillment. Scholars and rabbis opposed Hasidism, as the movement came to be known. The intellectual middle class also rejected it. They embraced the Haskalah, or Enlightenment movement, where reason, religious tolerance, and civil rights were stressed. This movement was the forerunner of nineteenth century Zionism, which urged Jews to return to their ancient homeland of Palestine.

In 1772, Russia, Austria, and Prussia each seized a portion of Poland, leaving only a small area surrounding Warsaw under Polish reign. When Poland achieved independence in 1919, much of the original territory was restored. Poland now had a population that included three million Jews.

The Nazis invaded Poland in September, 1939. Because Poland had a history of anti-Semitism, it was here the Germans chose to build the major death camps, such as Auschwitz and Majdanek. The Poles cooperated with the Nazis in rounding up the Jews. Thousands of Jews were marched under heavy guard into the forests and forced to dig their own graves. Millions more were herded into ghettos to await deportation to the gas chambers.

A total of 2,650,000 million Jews from all over Europe perished on Polish soil. With the death of Eastern European Jewry, an ancient community, rich in tradition and intellectual achievement, came to an end.

A year after World War II ended, 41 Jews, who had returned to their native city of Kielce, were murdered in the Jewish community center. Others, who had hoped to return to their former homes, realized they would not be welcomed and fled. Today, the number of Jews living in Poland is unknown. Figures vary between 4,000 and 35,000. Of these, only a handful of old men can be found in the Warsaw synagogue on Friday nights.

The Long Night

Marya (Stella) was an infant when the Nazis captured Poland. She spent the first six years of her life in hiding and in darkness. It was not until the Russians liberated her village in Poland that she learned of her true identity.

EVEN today, when I walk into a Catholic Church, I have ambivalent feelings. For six years, the only time I saw daylight was when I attended mass. The brilliance of the sunlight and the dazzling interior of the church became one in my mind. To be Catholic was to be warm and protected.

On the day in 1944 when the Russians marched into our village and liberated us from the Nazi rule, my mother took me aside.

"Stella Machusko is not your real name, and you are not Catholic," she told me.

At seven, this was difficult to understand. "What is my real name?"

"Marya Glindinski."

I put down the little Russian flag I had been waving. The excitement of the parade had evaporated. "And if I'm not Catholic, what am I?"

"A Jew."

"A Jew!" I had seen those creatures with their yellow stars, but they had all vanished, like my grandmother.

I ran to the mirror and inspected myself. "But I can't be a Jew. I don't have a yellow star or horns." I felt my nose with my index finger. "My nose is straight and my hair is blonde. You are wrong."

"Marya, we are Jews. If we had not pretended to be Catholic, we would have been killed."

"I won't be a Jew," I said, grasping her arms with my small hands. "I have to make my first communion. Aunt Nada is making me my white dress."

"Marya, we are what we are. You are a Jew."

I released my mother and started to scream. "If I am a Jew, I can never go to heaven. I shall burn." I brushed past her and ran to church. I tugged on the bell of the confessional box.

The priest entered. "Calm yourself, child. Nothing can be so terrible." He talked in a soothing voice until my sobs stopped. Reassured, I repeated what my mother had told me.

His voice hardened. "You are right. Jews do not go to heaven. They burn. You are not a Catholic. Leave."

I fell to the floor, my hand pressing my cross into my chest. As I lay on the floor, memories I had never understood returned.

I had always admired my grandmother's silver mesh purse and had begged her to give it to me. She would laugh and say, "Later, you're too young."

One day, before I could ask, she handed it to me. Kissing me, she walked out the door. All afternoon I waited for her, but she never came back.

Polish Jews rounded up by the Germans.

From some faraway place I remembered throngs of people. My mother and I were being pushed onto a train. Mother screamed, "Hold the child." I thought she said, "Jump." I jumped. She followed. We rolled down an embankment. Somehow we made our way back to Nada's house, where she hid us behind a false cupboard.

In a daze, I tried to interpret these recollections, but they made no sense. I had to find my mother and understand.

She was waiting on the steps of the church. "Marya, we are what we are," she repeated. "I shall tell you our story."

We walked down the dirt road towards the home of Nada, who had sheltered us — not really my aunt, but a neighbor.

"In 1939, your father, a doctor, left us to join the Polish army. On the way he stopped to say good-bye to his parents, who lived in a Russian section of Poland. The Russians, who were German allies then, seized him and sent him to Siberia."

"I have a father?" I interrupted. "I thought we had made him up. All those nights in the cellar, I wondered what it would be like to have a father. Why didn't you tell me?"

"It was too dangerous. You were only a year old when he left. I realized that our village in Carpathia was not safe. I bought false papers and fled with you to Nada. She lived not far from the Czechoslovakian border. Because you were so small, I was afraid you would reveal our hiding place, if you were up and about and playing. I had to keep you drugged during the day. Sometimes, when a more lenient German commander was in charge, we pretended that you were Nada's niece. It was during those times that you were allowed to go to church."

"I liked it then," I recalled. "We put our down quilts against the tile stove and were warm at night. Once, when soldiers burst into the house, you tied a rag around my neck. Then you sprinkled carbolic acid all around the bed. I had a hard time trying not to giggle when you said, '*cronk, cronk*' (sick, sick) and the soldiers fled because they thought I was sick."

Mother glanced at the cherry trees leading to Nada's. "After the fall of the Warsaw Ghetto, the Nazis intensified their search for Jews. The cupboard with its false back was no longer safe. We went back to living in the cellar."

I shuddered as I remembered the cellars in which we had hidden. Every time a trap door opened, my mother would draw me into a corner and wait. Often, a "cousin" would silently lead us through the starless night to another damp, dirt-floored cellar. Pigs, who were also being hidden from the Nazis, would share our evil-smelling quarters. If we were lucky, we found rotten potatoes under the straw. Some nights, we went to bed hungry. We slept on wooden planks covered with straw. I would amuse myself by chasing the rats and mice, or by rolling stones across the floor. All the seasons seemed the same without daylight.

One night, when I was five, Nada and a "cousin" came and took me to a convent. At daybreak, someone roused me. I blinked, my eyes unused to light. The nun led me to a beautiful chapel where we prayed. Nada had taught me the Hail Marys. After the Polish winters in the cellars, the convent was warm and lovely. There was sunshine and day and night. I had just begun to learn to read when my mother and a "cousin" came late one evening, and we vanished again into another cellar. This one was crowded with escaped prisoners of war.

Aside from the stay at the convent, the only other time I was permitted to go about in the daylight was during infrequent visits to church. After the darkness, nothing could be more exciting than the beautiful robes, the golden, jewelled chalice, and the sweet sounds of choir boys singing. I thought it was a dreadful shame that mother "had trouble with her knees" and could not come and kneel with me.

As we approached Nada's house, Mother paused at the iron gate. "Now our hiding is finished. Our Russian friends have rescued us. We can enjoy the daylight, and you can go to school."

I looked at the tiny brass eagles sitting inside on the windowsills. "You would never let me play with them."

Mother smiled. "No, they were signals for the Polish underground. When they were turned sideways, it was a sign that it was safe to come to Nada's house."

A big army truck had pulled in front of the gate. Russian soldiers hopped out and began hauling office files up the path. We started to follow.

"Who are you?" A soldier stopped us with the point of his bayonet.

"We live here," Mother replied.

"Go in. This is now the headquarters of the Russian Command."

We went to Nada's room. "What is happening?" Mother asked.

"The Russians have taken over the house. No one is allowed to leave." Nada was very upset.

"We are prisoners again?" Mother asked, the creases in her forehead appearing.

"Yes."

"Marya," my mother said. I looked around to see who she was talking to. "Marya, Stella, remember when the Germans once found us in the kitchen and we said that Daddy was a prisoner of the Russians in Siberia?"

"Yes," I answered. "But I thought we just pretended I had a father."

"Now you know you do, but to please the Russians,

we must say now that he is in a German concentration camp."

I nodded. Somehow, I knew not to ask any questions.

After a few weeks under Russian rule, my mother told me we were going to play a game, "so we can find your father."

A Russian soldier came into the room and began to put straw into the bottom of several huge wooden crates. Then he packed china and bowls along the sides and bottom.

I watched, wondering what the straw had to do with the game. When the crate was half full, Mother held out her hand. "We are going to pretend to be china. And no matter what happens, you are not to say one word. This nice soldier will pack you in one box and me in another." She handed me a glass of liquid. "Here, take this to make you sleepy."

Hours later, I was jolted awake by a huge bump. I tried to rub my eyes, but there was straw all over my face. I peeked through the wooden slats. All I could see were other crates. They rattled with each bump in the mountain road. After a long time, we stopped. Someone climbed onto the back of the truck. I heard a man tap one of the boxes.

"Open it," he said. The Russian driver lifted the top and pulled out some dishes.

"Okay," the inspector said. "On your way."

After a few more miles, the truck stopped. I saw soldiers opening the other crates. They had smuggled fifteen of us across the Polish border into Czechoslovakia. We got out of the crates.

"Good luck reaching Austria," the soldiers said, as they handed us kielbasa and black bread.

After twelve days of subsisting on raw potatoes and sleeping in the fields, our ragged, rain-soaked group straggled into the United Nations Refugee Assistance center in Vienna. The officials took away our clothing and sprayed us with disinfectant, to get rid of the lice.

I looked around at the others in the UNRRA camp. Aside from a brief time at the convent, I had never been with other children. And these were Jews! What was wrong with them — they didn't even understand Polish! I turned my back. A little girl rolled a ball at me. We began to play.

Through a miracle, my father was alive. A general amnesty had freed him from Siberia, and he had joined the British Army. His combat unit was in Italy. When my mother contacted him, he sent an ambulance to Austria to pick us up.

In May 1946, at the age of eight, I met my father for the first time. He kissed me and handed me a doll with blue eyes and eyelashes that moved up and down. It was my first doll.

The former Stella Machuska is married to an American. They have two children and live in the Eastern United States.

When the Jews were expelled from Spain in 1492, large numbers of them fled to Amsterdam. Although Holland was under Spanish rule, the local Dutch rulers were less intent on persecuting the Jews.

Many of these refugees were Marranos, Jews who, given the choice between death and conversion to Christianity in the fourteenth and fifteenth centuries, had outwardly become Christians. A great number of these Marranos remained secret Jews, surreptitiously following Judaism and passing the religious traditions on to their children.

When the Dutch gained their independence from Spain in the seventeenth century, the government became more tolerant, and Jews were allowed to build a synagogue. With the arrival of more Jews from Austria and Germany, two groups emerged: the Sephardic (descended from Spanish refugees) and the Ashkenazic (descended from Polish and German refugees).

Jews in Holland prospered, and in 1796, they gained full rights as citizens. By the twentieth century, Jews held important positions in Dutch society.

There were 140,000 Jews living in Holland by 1939. They felt safe; Holland had been neutral during World War I and would no doubt remain so in the event of a second world war. When Germany attacked Poland in 1939, Holland again announced its neutrality.

But on May 10, 1940, thousands of Germans landed by parachute on Dutch soil. German tanks and foot soldiers followed. By January 1941, the Germans had forced all Jews to register. The following month, Dutch Nazis attacked the old Jewish section in Amsterdam. Christian neighbors helped the Jews to fight back.

A few days later, 425 young Jews were sent to Buchenwald concentration camp in Germany. This prompted Dutch dockworkers to call for a general strike in protest on February 25, 1941. Given the five-thousand-year-old history of persecution of the Jews around the world, this was a remarkable demonstration. Citizens of all economic classes, from stockbrokers to fishermen, joined the dockworkers. For three days the streets and canals lay empty. The strike was crushed by the arrest of 3,500 people.

Nevertheless, the Dutch continued to aid the Jews. In this flat, crowded country with few natural hiding places, 20,000 Jews were concealed by their countrymen. Some

10,000 were discovered — usually with fatal consequences for both fugitive and protector. Of the pre-war Jewish population of 140,000, 105,000 were annihilated.

The
Great
Commandment

Pieter Timmerman was a fourteen-year-old schoolboy the day the Nazis invaded Holland by parachute in 1940. Soon after, he became a member of the Dutch Resistance.

I was fourteen when the Nazis marched into Holland. When the schools reopened, we found the Jewish teachers had been dismissed.

"No Jewish teachers, no school!" we shouted on the steps. "They are Dutchmen."

One of the teachers who had been dismissed came up to us. "Pieter, Piet, Annalise, Jan, please go inside. You cannot help us. You can only hurt yourselves." Nothing my instructor said made any sense that day. Why couldn't I help and act as my conscience dictated?

Although my family wasn't Jewish, many of our friends were. We had never separated people into religious categories. As a "shabbas goy," I frequently turned on the lights and lighted the stove for Jewish friends on the Sabbath. Whether Jews or Protestants or Catholics, we were all Dutchmen. Did not the Protestant Church emphasize the "Grote Gebod" or Great Commandment: *Love thy neighbor as thyself.* All my life I had followed this rule . . . why should I be forced to stop now?

Despite my appearance as a schoolboy, I began to carry messages for the Resistance, reporting on German troop movements. I knew that I would be called up for forced labor when I turned eighteen. If I could only obtain a boat, I thought, I could sail from the North Sea to England and escape.

What would be a small, inconspicuous seaworthy boat? An Eskimo kayak! Though I had seen one only in books, I set about to build one. Since our local library had no books with detailed drawings, I sent to Austria for diagrams. A friend who owned a lumberyard gave me wood, and I gathered metal from an allied aircraft that had been shot down. Night after night I shaped and molded the ribs

Grim cartoon in Metro, *oldest underground newspaper in The Netherlands. Caption reads: Seyss Inquart (German commissioner of The Netherlands): "The caring, responsible and patient treatment that The Netherlands has received for the past four years will not be possible anymore."*

for the kayak until I had a seaworthy craft. All I needed was a waterproof cover. For months I searched for some. Finally, I admitted defeat and gave up.

When I was eighteen I received a notice to report for an examination so I could be drafted for forced labor. It was considered a disgrace to work for the Germans. Many tried to avoid service, but I didn't know how.

In the waiting room I noticed that none of the doctors or nurses came from my village. As I slouched in my chair I recalled my mother's nagging, "If you don't sit up straight and wipe that foolish grin off your face, people will take you for an idiot."

Now I had a plan. I sprawled all over the chair, and when my name was called, I pretended not to hear. It was called again. I kept swinging my foot against the bar of the chair.

A man tapped me on the shoulder. "We are calling you."

Looking bewildered, I stood up and allowed him to lead me to the nurse's station.

"What is your name?" she asked.

I stared at her blankly.

"What is your name?" she asked again.

"Oh, oh, you wwwant to know mmmmy nnname?" I bobbed my head up and down. "Wwwwhen I wwwas smmmalll mmmmy mmmother ccccalled mme babbby. Bbbut nnnow sssshe calls mmmee — " I stopped, as if to remember what she did call me, "— sssson." I smiled, very pleased with myself.

Impatiently, she asked me another question. "What grade did you go to in school?"

"School? Ththththere is a schhhol on the rrroad near Mr. Ccccas' house. It is vvvverry fffarr." I brushed my hand across my nose and wiped it on my pants.

The nurse stood up and pushed me into the examining area. "Take off your shoes," she said, drawing the curtain closed.

I loudly dropped one shoe to the floor.

"Just put the other one down quietly," she scolded.

I slammed the other one down.

Hurriedly, the doctor placed me in front of the eye chart. He pointed to an "A."

"Thhhhree," I yelled.

He pointed to a four.

"Aaaaaaugst," I said, clapping my hands rapidly. The ear test produced the same catastrophe. When he whispered one number in my ear, I stammered three different ones.

They handed me my shoes and shoved me towards the door. "We are very sorry, but we cannot use you. Please do not be too disappointed."

When the Burgomaster or mayor of our town, a Nazi sympathizer, heard I had been rejected he was furious. "One day the scores will be evened for the Timmerman family. The father is no better."

Now I was forced to hide out. My father found a safe place for me on the farm of a man known for his pro-Nazi sympathies. One day while I was working on the farm, Father was picked up in a raid. During the raid the Nazis pushed Mother down the stairs. She suffered a concussion.

I decided to risk sneaking home; there was no one to care for my mother and little sister.

At the farmhouse before ours, I stumbled on German troops and came face to face with a soldier about my age.

"Halt, where are you going?"

"My mother is ill. I work on a farm. I'm trying to slip through curfew to see her," I said.

He put his gun at my back. "All right," he said in a low voice, "I'll take you home. If anyone stops us, just say we're taking things to your house." I prayed he would not stumble.

We reached my house, and he motioned me towards the door and left. My little sister ran out to greet me. "Pieter," she cried. "Mother is very sick. I am so glad you are here now to help."

On another evening, I rode my bicycle home. A man, wearing an American flyer's uniform, stepped out of the woods. It would be hard to help him; all activities in the Resistance had ceased since a betrayal earlier that week. I finally made arrangements to bring him to another contact. At first, I thought I should get him civilian clothes. With so many Germans around, I decided against it. "If you're captured, you'll be treated as a prisoner of war if you are in uniform."

The drizzling rain blotted out the new moon. We stumbled into every bush and tree but safely passed the first roadblock. As we continued on the muddy road, I bumped into two Germans coming home with girls.

"Halt, who are you?" one called, touching my woolen jacket.

"I'm a farmhand on my way home. I had to work late."

"All right. Go on and hurry."

I reached for the American's hand and pushed him forward. His flight boots slapped against the mud, each step cutting into the sand with a heavy thud.

"Halt, who is with you?" the Germans demanded.

"A deaf and dumb man."

The German soldier stuck out his hand and felt the American's fur collar. We were discovered.

As a prisoner of war, the American pilot was offered a cigarette and treated correctly by the SS officer. I had to stand facing the wall while the Nazis checked my identity.

They brought me to the local authorities. "You made a good catch," the mayor said. "This boy is a member of the underground and a malingerer. His whole family is rotten."

"So, you are the rotten son of a rotten father," the SS officer said, kicking me in the face. "Rotten eggs get broken." He punched me until I dropped to the floor, unconscious.

Someone threw cold water on me. I blinked and looked up. The SS officer, a lieutenant, sat sprawled on a chair, smoking a cigarette, waiting for me to come to. He stood up and ground the lit cigarette into my arm.

"Where were you going?"

"I don't know."

His blows tore open my cheek. "What is the name of your contact?"

"I don't know."

"Talk boy, or we'll hang you in the marketplace and blackbirds will pick out your eyes." He slapped me so hard my glasses fell off my face.

"I do not know. I do not know."

"Eighteen years old and he won't talk. Take him to Schroyder. He'll get it out of him."

I reached for the parts of my glasses and put them into my pocket. Four soldiers, their bayonets touching my back, marched me through the empty streets, past my house and our church to the train station, but no one saw me. Just before the train pulled out, I spotted a classmate who waved. I drew a finger across my throat as the open boxcar in which I was riding jerked forward. I was being taken to Germany for interrogation.

Schroyder lived up to his reputation as one of the most degenerate and vicious SS men. After he had worked me over, I signed a statement, my eyes too bloodshot to focus on the print, my brain too fogged to comprehend what I was signing. Most importantly, I had not revealed the name of my contact.

I lay on the floor of a narrow cell, exhausted. Empty of hope, I was in a daze. Beautiful dreams of sailing with my father on the river drifted through my sleep. I woke up. There must be a way to escape.

I picked the threads of my torn coat and knotted them together to make one strong thread. Then I tied the lens to the frame of my glasses. Now that I could see, I tried to pick the cell lock but couldn't. Discouraged, I fell asleep.

My cellmate, Willie Hoya, had been a critic of the Nazis since 1922 and had spent most of his life in prison as a result. He offered me advice. "Always remember two things. Whatever you do, never confide in anyone you meet in prison. And always believe that what you are doing is right."

The Nazis transferred me to another cell. My new cellmate told me details of his underground activities. I listened, and remembering Willie's advice, talked about sailing trips.

The Nazis gave up hope of breaking me. "You will be shot tonight," the guard told me when he brought the rancid soup. "A transport will take you to Munster."

Doors slammed. Trembling, I waited through the night. God, oh my God, why am I so helpless to save myself? I am eighteen-years-old. After tonight — no more!

When a rim of morning light edged the high window, the guard unlocked the door. "You are lucky," he told me. "Your transport had to be used for new prisoners. You can live a few more days."

A few more days? What difference did it make?

Although I could not know it, the classmate who had seen me in the open boxcar had informed the Resistance. Mr. Laidermann, the manager of a textile factory, and Mr. Hoppes, manager of a municipal waterworks, had been following me from jail to jail hoping to barter for my freedom.

When they got to see Colonel Schroyder, they placed two bottles of jenever on his desk and toasted Schroyder,

Hitler, and a German victory. After an hour of this drunken camaraderie, Mr. Laidermann pulled out his order book. "Do you want any textiles?" he asked Colonel Schroyder.

"No, but my wife does," he answered.

As Laidermann wrote up the order, he asked casually, "Do you have a Timmerman in your custody?"

"No," said the colonel, "I have never heard of him."

Mr. Hoppes poured the colonel another jenever. "A foolish, adventuresome adolescent. He's harmless. By the way, does your wife like Chinese silk?"

"She adores it," Schroyder said. "I'll check my files and see if that Timmerman is here." He rang for his secretary. "Is there a Timmerman boy in the files?"

"Don't you remember?" she asked. "The commandant was here an hour ago. The boy is to be hanged." She bowed and left.

"I am sorry," Schroyder said. "If I had the papers, I could have destroyed them and the prisoner would cease to exist. Now there is nothing I can do. He must be executed tonight." He stood and raised his hand. "I look forward to the receipt of the textiles for my wife. Heil Hitler!"

As Hoppes and Laidermann rose to go, the door opened and the commandant returned. "I forgot something."

The two businessmen produced more bottles of jenever. "We drink to your health." Laidermann pulled out the textile order book.

"Would you like some textiles?" he asked the commandant.

"No, but my wife would." The commandant ordered thousands of dollars of scarce materials.

And, after more drinks and toasts, it was agreed that the papers of Pieter Timmerman, an inconsequential, mischievous lad, would be destroyed.

The guard unlocked my cell. "You are to go to the Colonel. He is personally taking care of your case."

I trembled as they led me outside the prison to the garage. Why couldn't they hang me without another beating?

"Get in the back," Schroyder ordered me, as his chauffeur opened the door of the Mercedes. "We will drive you home."

I felt better; to die in one's own country did not seem as futile as to die on foreign soil. At the border I was told to lie on the floor. Soon after the chauffeur parked the Mercedes next to another car — Mr. Laidermann's.

"Crawl into the back seat of that car," Schroyder commanded.

I did as I was told. Was Schroyder going to shoot me and leave me in this car? I heard the door slam and the Mercedes drive off. I lay there, uncomprehending, afraid to move.

In a few minutes Mr. Laidermann got into the car and drove me home. I hid in a crawl space. Until I knew for sure that my papers had been destroyed, I could be captured again. Nightmares shook my sleep. I dreamt I was standing on a platform waiting to be executed, blackbirds circling around my head. Every night I woke up shouting, "I do not know. I do not know."

Weeks later, Mr. Laidermann informed me my papers were officially destroyed. I had to "dive" or go underground. I joined a group of Dutch boys in the forced labor system. Because we crossed the border every night, we continued to work with the Resistance. We were not counted very carefully, and we smuggled prisoners out among us.

When the Nazis became suspicious, we were told laborers could no longer cross the border into Holland every evening. I had to escape. A sympathetic doctor examined me. He stamped my name on someone else's X-rays. "Worker has T.B. He should be sent home."

I climbed on my bicycle and headed home. Pedaling down a back road, I saw German guards standing in the middle of my path. I could not avoid them.

Driving straight up to them I stopped. "Excuse me," I said. "I'm the new farmhand. Could you tell me the way to the farmhouse?" They drew a map in the dirt.

Memorial to the Dutch dock workers who led the strike against the Germans.

I reached home safely. Months later, Holland was liberated by English and Canadian troops. I was finally free.

Pieter Timmerman's personal recovery took a long time. "Unable to tolerate being in a closed room, I had to give up my lifelong dream of becoming a naval architect." Today, Pieter is a successful advertising executive. He and his wife and two daughters live happily in Amsterdam. Pieter still has stored in his garage the metal pipes that were to form the kayak for his escape to freedom.

Jews entered Belgium with Julius Caesar. They established themselves as traders in spices from the Orient. Only a fragment of the Jewish community in Belgium survived the massacres of the Crusades during the Middle Ages. Later, in the sixteenth century, Marranos, fleeing Portugal, established the diamond trade in Antwerp, making that city a major diamond exchange.

Belgium, which had been under Spanish and French rule, became part of the Austrian Netherlands in 1814. When Belgium gained independence in 1830, equal rights were granted to all citizens. Many Polish and Russian Jews, attracted by the liberal atmosphere, came to Belgium.

Belgium attempted to remain neutral in World War I, but that neutrality was violated when German troops invaded Belgium en route to France. In 1939, Belgium once again announced its neutrality, but German troops invaded the country on May 10, 1940.

Belgian authorities, who were charged by the Nazis with enforcing anti-Jewish measures, refused to do so. After a German order required all Jews to wear the Yellow Star of David, thousands of Belgians paraded in the streets with six-pointed stars decorated in the national colors of black, yellow and red.

Cardinal van Roey denounced the persecution of Jews and sent a message to the Vatican asking the Pope to intervene. The Pope did not respond, but the Belgian clergy helped to hide three thousand Jewish children and ten thousand Jewish adults.

An active resistance movement, Front de L'Independence, organized escape routes to Switzerland and Spain. Unlike the Germans and the Austrians who cooperated with the Nazis, the Belgians often sabotaged efforts to deport Jews. The doors of train transports to the concentration camps were left open. On one occasion, saws were smuggled into the cattle cars so the deportees could escape.

Out of a pre-war population of 90,000 Jews, 20,000 returned to Belgium after World War II. Jewish exiles from other countries were also welcomed to this small, over-crowded nation.

Sanctuary Among the Enemy

Alex was six years old when the British evacuated Dunkirk, near the Belgian border. I interviewed him one rainy evening in Pennsylvania.

"What do you want to know?" he asked.

"Everything," I said. "What was it like to be a small boy then?"

The six-foot-two man became a child. He started to cry. "I'm sorry," he said. "I can't talk to you." After a while he recovered. "I'm all right now," he said and told me his story.

THERE was definitely going to be a war. My father thought we would be safe in our summer house near Dunkirk, on the French-Belgian border. With a cellar stocked with potatoes, onions, and turnips, my two brothers and I stayed there with a governess. My parents came from Antwerp to see us every weekend.

On May 9, 1940, we went to bed, expecting to see our parents the next day. In the middle of the night, the shrill sound of a siren jolted me from sleep. Terrifying explosions shook the floors and windows. My brothers — ages eight and five — crept into my bed, and we huddled together.

The next day we stood in front of the window and waited. Where were our parents? Would we be abandoned? At dusk they appeared, exhausted and frenzied. They bundled us into the car, a Peugeot, and headed for France where we were to meet our relatives, who were also fleeing the Nazis. From France we hoped to go through Spain to Portugal where we might obtain visas for America.

When my brother and I came down with the German measles, the escape was halted. Twenty-six people would have to wait until we recovered. My father sent for the local French doctor.

"As mayor of this town, I cannot see traitors," he said. Then he added, "But as a physician, I shall come after five p.m."

When we recovered, we moved to Marseille, France. My uncle in New York sent an affidavit saying he would be responsible for us if we came to America. But the quota was filled, so he arranged for us to go to the Philippines.

First we had to get to Lisbon, Portugal, via Spain to board a ship. The Spanish consul issued visas for my mother and us, but would not issue one for our father. The Spanish feared he would join Allied Forces. Father insisted we go ahead, promising he'd find a way to get to Lisbon.

Father made his way to Morocco and then to Tangiers. "Only a serious illness in your family will get you a visa to Lisbon," the sympathetic Portuguese consul told him. "Your wife will have to send me a telegram."

Mother was superstitious and did not want to send my father a telegram, even if it was fake. "It's like putting a curse on the family," she wrote. But after a month she wired: "Children sick. Come immediately."

Life in Manila was hot but pleasant. Then, on December 7, 1941, the sounds of bombs disturbed my sleep once again. "I'm having a nightmare about Belgium," I thought. The terrible sounds continued.

My parents ran into the living room and turned on the radio. "Pearl Harbor has been bombed. The Japanese are attacking Manila."

Where could we go? There were no trains or borders left. Some Filipinos fled inland in horse-drawn carts. Americans and Europeans stayed put and dug fox holes in their gardens. There were no air raid shelters. Fires blazed throughout the area. Houses near the military installations disintegrated into charred wood. Hulls of sunken ships lay in the bay.

I watched the triumphant entrance of the Japanese. A five-car caravan of officers whizzed by. Behind them followed groups of soldiers in red and yellow buses shouting, "Banzai!" and waving their flag, the Rising Sun. I waved and shouted, "Banzai!" To a seven-year-old the noise and commotion of a parade is always fun.

The Japanese victory quickly changed our lives. They requisitioned our apartment and we were sent to a detention camp, set up on a former university campus. We slept wherever we could find room — on the floor, in the closets, in the restrooms. Father had to wear a red armband with black Japanese characters that said: "National Enemy."

Despite everyone's efforts, many of us suffered from dysentery, including myself and my brothers. The Japanese, who were fond of children, told us we would be temporarily released. We were regarded as allies, since Germany occupied Belgium, and Japan was allied with Germany. I learned, very early, when stopped by a soldier to say, "I am a Belgian."

There was open hostility between the German Nazis and the Jews living in Manila. One day, during siesta, Eric, my brother, was riding his scooter (that Father had fashioned from two pieces of wood and a roller skate) in front of the home of a Nazi. Infuriated, the woman rushed outside, pushed Eric to the ground and seized the scooter. Eric ran down the street howling. A Japanese soldier stopped him, and Eric managed, in Japanese, English and sign language, to tell him what had happened.

The soldier took Eric by the hand and led him to his company. The men, grabbing their rifles, marched with Eric in the lead to the house of the Nazi.

The sergeant knocked on the door. The woman opened it and stared out at the fixed bayonets and the small boy. Silently, she handed over the scooter. Then the Japanese soldiers stood on the sidewalk while Eric noisily rode his scooter up and down in the sleepy Manila afternoon.

On February 7, 1945, the telephone rang. Father answered it. "Our friends are here," the voice on the other end said. Father turned on the radio. There was music, then silence. We heard the boom of guns. Outside, the blue Manila sky had turned black as thousands of American planes flew across the horizon.

Day after day the reports of hand-to-hand fighting came through over the radio. The Japanese had vowed to fight to the death.

We lived in the only suburban area that was not affected by the fighting. One day the door bell rang. Friends from the city stood there, their clothing torn and covered with ashes.

"How nice to see you," I said, automatically the polite and formal Belgian schoolboy. They stared at me in disbelief.

Soon others followed to share the safety of our house and our meager rice-bread rations.

The Americans finally took the city after bitter fighting. Among the casualties was the synagogue.

At Passover all Jews were invited to a seder. Army jeeps picked up the guests and delivered them to the race track. For the first time in six years we sat at a table covered by a white cloth and laden with matzah, gefilte fish, and horseradish sauce.

Our tattered clothes and wartime bruises faded in the starlit night as the high, sweet voice of a five-year-old asked the ancient question that begins the Passover ceremony: "Why is this night different from all other nights?"

Today Alex is a university professor. He lives in the United States.

THE UKRAINE

The Ukraine, which is now a part of southwestern Russia, was inhabited by Jewish traders before the birth of Christ. Their caravans established the spice and cloth routes between the Orient and Eastern Europe.

There had even been a Jewish ruler, Bulan, in the Ukraine between the eighth and ninth centuries. When Bulan was defeated by the Russians, the Jews fled. Then, in the eleventh century, German Jews, fleeing the Crusaders' swords, came to the Ukraine, which was now under Polish rule. More refugees from Germany followed in the fourteenth century, when Jews were blamed and attacked for causing the Black Death or bubonic plague that had stricken Europe. These

Jews of German descent, the Ashkenazis, helped to colonize the vast lands of the Ukraine and prospered.

The ravages of the Cossacks in the seventeenth century wiped out Jewish communities in the Ukraine, as well as in Poland. When Russia seized part of the Ukraine in 1772, Czar Nicholas the First issued an edict limiting Jewish settlement to those cities in which they already lived. This area was known as "The Pale of Settlement."

In 1827, the Czar decreed that all male Jews between 12 and 25 years had to serve in the Russian army for 25 years. The Russian army paid child snatchers to take young boys from their families. Since the Russian army denied Jews the opportunity to observe their religious laws and customs, many Jews felt that conscription was the same as murder. Jewish boys cut off their "trigger" fingers or punctured their ear drums to escape the draft. Some escaped to America.

Persecutions against the Jews continued throughout the nineteenth and twentieth centuries under the Czar.

In 1941, the Germans defied the Nazi-Soviet Non-Aggression Pact of 1939 and invaded the Ukraine. They immediately began their round-up of Jews. Andrei Pshetitsky, the head of the Uniate Church of Lvov, urged his monks and nuns to hide Jewish children. His was a rare protest. Many Ukrainians eagerly joined the Nazis in carrying out their planned annihilation of the Jews.

Prior to World War II one and a half million Jews lived in the Ukraine. When Hitler attacked, many fled. The exact number of Jews still living in the Ukraine is difficult to estimate because the Russians do not keep records of religious affiliations. They do, however, stamp the passports of known Jews with a J.

Rachel's Wedding

Robert was eleven years old and living in Wlodziemierz, a town in the Ukraine, when the Russians invaded in 1939. A year later he became a fugitive from the Nazis.

When I asked to interview him, his wife protested. "He'll start having night-mares all over again."

"I want to talk to her," he replied. "Young people must know."

"**S**IT down on the side of the bed, Robert, and give me your hand." My grandfather's wrinkled arm reached out and clasped my chubby fingers. We had shared many secrets and stories, and I sensed that this would be the last time.

"Listen to me, Robert. You are only eleven years old, but you must understand that bad times are coming for our people. As you grow older, there may be a time when to survive or to save someone else you will be forced to dance to music you don't like. Do it! Don't commit the sin in your heart, but pretend to do it."

My grandfather closed his eyes. A few weeks later, the Germans marched into Poland, and the Russians, allied with Germany, seized our part of the Ukraine. With no radio or newspapers, I had never heard of the Nazis or their philosophies.

Until the Russian occupation, my life had been a happy one. Father was in the fruit business, and every year he would rent fruit trees before they bloomed. When the orchards were ripe, he would pay farmers to harvest the fruit. I still remember the smells and the sight of wagonload after wagonload, always with clusters of bees, rolling up to the door of our warehouse. From there, the fruit would be shipped all over Europe.

The peasants loved my father. If someone lost a cow, for instance, my father would loan the man money to buy another, even if it would take him twenty years to repay the debt.

My Aunt Golda's wedding lasted for two days. Carts and wagons came from miles around. Everyone drank and danced and toasted the long life of the bride and groom. No

With the few possessions they were allowed, people await deportation to the concentration camps.

one knew that this wedding would be the last celebration our family would share together.

When the Russians marched into Wlodziemierz, my hometown, beating their drums, they seized my father as a "collaborator." His crime? He was the head of the Jewish community. His punishment? A choice between Siberia, execution, or jail. The peasants went to the commandant and obtained his release. When I look back, the Russian occupation seems benign.

Without warning on June 22, 1941, German artillery shells shot across the Bug River and scored direct hits on the homes of my four uncles. My father and I ran outside to help, but the landscape was a nightmare of torsos, hands, heads, arms, legs, and fists. There was no time to bury the fragments.

The Germans ordered all Jews to assemble in the town square. Aunt Golda, of the joyous wedding, nine-months pregnant, could not move quickly enough in the hot sun for the Nazi lieutenant. He kicked her in the belly and sent her sprawling. With his bayonet he ripped her stomach open. The whole village was forced to stand there and watch her bleed to death: Yankle, a six-foot giant; Chaim, her husband; my father, and my five-year-old sister Rachel.

The peasants helped us escape that evening from our barbed-wire enclosure. We fled thirteen miles to the Bug River, where we crossed into the Russian zone. We existed on unripened corn, berries, and mushrooms. But, as the first frost fell, my father took me aside.

"Robert, we must make a pact. If times get too bad, I shall kill Mother and you are to kill Rachel. Then we shall kill each other. I know it is hard for you to understand, but there are things worse than death."

Rachel had followed us. She started to cry. "You are not to do that. One day you will dance at my wedding. If we're going to die, let the Germans do it."

When the weather grew colder, the peasants hid my mother and Rachel. Father and I remained in the woods, sleeping in caves.

One day, a Lithuanian guerrilla soldier cornered us. "Jews, come with me."

"What are you going to do with us?" Father asked. He had rented fruit trees from this boy's father.

"Don't be frightened," Berco whispered. "I had to stop you. My group is watching from the woods." He prodded Father with his gun. "I'll turn you over to the leader. Then tonight I'll help you escape. Look frightened, but don't worry. I love you too much to kill you."

A few months later, we were not so lucky. Another group of bounty hunters captured us and for a few dollars turned us over to the Germans. My father and I were separated and put into concentration camps.

Like ants, the other prisoners and I carried bags of grain on our backs up a steep, slanted plank to a grain bin. The sack in front of me had a hole, and grain trickled out. I slipped. Pains shot through my ankle, but I got up. To remain on the floor would mean death. All day I tried to ignore the pain, but at nightfall, I could scarcely limp back to the barracks.

A doctor who was in my work group examined me. "Robert will have to stay off his feet for a month. How can we hide him?" he asked the others as he tore apart his only shirt to bandage me.

"In the ground," said an engineer. "I'll design a cover that will hide him but permit him to breathe."

My tired and starving work group began to dig a hole. By bartering their few possessions, they obtained boards to make a cover. I climbed into the pit, wondering if I would come out alive. At night, the lid was kept open. At each roll call, someone answered to my name. The entire barracks had taken a terrible risk.

When I recovered, I found that we had a new work detail: digging holes. Deep, deep pits, four of them, large enough to execute and bury twenty-five hundred people at one time. My grandfather's words came back to me: "There may be a time when you will be forced to dance in order to survive. Do it." My shovel bit into the earth as we dug four smaller holes at the corner of the larger ones.

Orthodox Jews wept as they were forced to undress. Exposing their bodies was considered worse than death. The Nazis doused them with kerosene and pushed them into the holes. Then set them on fire.

I had to escape. I backed away. Let a bullet stop me, but not this. The Germans had come out to enjoy the spectacle. I waited until the beams from the revolving searchlight were on the other side of the camp and slipped through the gate.

In the forest, I joined a band of Russian partisans. My first mission was to help free a captured general. Posing as a shoeshine boy, I led the guerrilla soldiers towards the German

Partisans waged a constant underground warfare.

compound. When I bent down to shine the sentry's boots, one of my companions knifed him. The other sentry appeared. He, too, was killed. The partisans put on the German uniforms, and I preceded them into camp, shouting, "Shine, shoe shine."

After the partisans freed the general, they signaled me. Casually, I walked towards the gate. An alarm sounded. I dropped my shoe box and ran into the forest.

Each mission was thought of as our last. No one really cared. We knew we were doomed, and it was better to die fighting than in a fiery pit. One morning, I lay on my stomach and counted the number of tanks crawling up the hill. As I timed the distance between each tank, I noted where each mine had to be placed. German precision enabled us to blow up fifteen of their tanks. Again I fled into the forest. Three days after this successful mission, we were captured by bounty hunters.

Another camp! As a partisan, I was marked for instant death. I was lined up behind the others, single file, in front of a steel stretcher. Three people lay down on the stretcher. The Germans gave the order. The Jewish *Kapos*, prisoners who were forced to help the Nazis in the concentration camps, thrust the stretcher loaded with people into the oven. The next three victims advanced. I was fourth in line. A guard jerked my elbow and pulled me out. Men were needed to cut grain.

When the grain work detail returned to camp, I was missing. I hid in an attic, the sun beating against the clay shingles creating a temperature of 150 degrees. To keep from becoming dehydrated, I drank my urine. I was determined to leave there alive.

A few days later, I smuggled myself into the Warsaw Ghetto and joined the Jewish Fighting Organization. Until now, I had been merely flirting with death. This skirmish would surely be my last.

At fifteen, I became a captain. With spears, sticks, knives, homemade grenades, and pitifully few guns (the Polish Resistance refused to help us), we met the German tanks. We forced the Germans to divert troops from the battlefront to subdue our rag-tag army. From attic to attic, underground bunker to bunker, we hit, ran, and hit again.

We exploded an electric mine and killed one hundred Germans. The Nazis retaliated with machines that flooded our bunkers with gasoline and poison gas. Half-gassed, I dropped into the cold, filthy water of the sewer. The remaining members of the Warsaw Ghetto resisters crawled on their hands and knees through the blackness. For twenty hours we were without food and water. If we took a sip of the stinking water, we would die. We pushed and pulled one another forward. No one could think of what lay ahead when we reached the manhole at the Prosta-Twarda intersection. We got there and waited. Then someone lifted the cover from outside. The daylight stung my eyes. Bread and soup were passed down.

"Wait," a voice said. The top clanged into place.

The next night three Jews and a Pole hijacked a truck and drove it to the manhole. We stretched out our slime-

Captured Warsaw Ghetto fighters, 1943.

covered arms, and our rescuers pulled us, rung over rung, out of the sewers and on to the floor of the truck. My physical stupor could not quiet my mind. Why did I survive? How had I dared? I thought of what my grandfather had said. Was it worth it?

I slept for a week among the partisans in the Mlochini forest. They welcomed me as a demolitions expert. With my blond hair and ragged clothes, I looked like a Polish child. They sent me out to blow up a bridge.

"Bitte, brot (please, bread)," I wailed at the German sentry standing guard. He walked towards me, his gun slung over his shoulder. As he squatted down to talk to me, I thrust a knife into his heart and kicked his body into the water. After I blew up the bridge, I ran into the forest where bounty hunters found me and turned me over to the Germans.

Block 10, Auschwitz. Take a healthy fifteen-year-old male. Expose his body to X-rays and injections. See if his manhood can be destroyed. I fought the pains shooting through my spine and across my body. Every day, a man who had been trained as a doctor and had sworn an oath to preserve life, conducted his experiments and recorded the physical changes in my body. I was no longer considered a human being. I had to escape. Death on a barbed wire held more nobility.

Once again I found my way into the forest, and once again a "good" Lithuanian took a bounty in exchange for my body and soul and turned me over to the Germans. For eight days I endured the crazy, stinking, screaming world of a locked cattle car. Not too many of us reached Dachau alive, and I have blotted out of my memory most of my experiences in that death camp. How I survived, I cannot recall. That I did survive was miraculous. An American soldier told me the story later.

The Allies reached Dachau so swiftly that the Germans did not have time to burn the corpses. It was a bright sunny day, and the sergeant walked past the tens of thousands of bodies slung like piles of dung across the compound. As he passed the first group, he had this crazy feeling someone was watching him. He looked up and down the path. The grounds were empty of anything that was alive. No one else from his unit had had the stomach to inspect this macabre testimony

Concentration camp prisoners.

to the Nazis "final solution." He broke into a sweat and started to run. Something stopped him and drew him back.

The sergeant forced himself to look at the fleshless bodies. My eyes followed his movements, and he realized that someone was alive. He reached for my wrist and felt a slight pulse.

"Jesus Christ," he muttered, and separated me from the dead. The war was over. I had survived.

When I recovered, I contacted some friends from Wlodziemierz who had emigrated to America before the war. They brought me to America. The next year, I enlisted in the armed services. Since I knew nine languages, I was sent back to Europe as an interpreter. I was almost afraid to return, afraid that I would kill any German I met, on the spot. Yet, there was a chance that my parents had survived. I had to find out.

In Bremerhaven, I approached a Catholic priest. "Help me, please," I said. "I want to see if my parents are still alive."

"Why don't you go to a rabbi?" He picked up a stack of papers on his desk. "These are all requests from Catholic groups searching for survivors."

"I can't find a rabbi. You are a man of God. I ask your help regardless of my religion."

"Forgive me," he said, picking up the phone to make some inquiries. In a few minutes he handed me the keys to his car and German gas stamps. "Your parents are at a camp not far from here."

At the refugee camp gate, the guard was surly. "No Americans allowed here. We police ourselves."

"Hello, Simon," I said, recognizing my former schoolmate.

He stared at me. "Robert! Your parents and sister are here. They were here last week when you came to play soccer with your unit. We didn't recognize you."

I approached the building where my parents were living. A lovely blonde teenager sat on the steps.

She screamed, "Robert is here."

My mother rushed to the door and fainted.

Rachel and my parents emigrated to Canada. And one day, we fulfilled her prophesy. We danced at her wedding.

Unlike other victims of the experiments at Auschwitz, Block 10, Robert was later able to have children. He lives in Florida with his wife and six children.

FRANCE

After the destruction of the Temple in Palestine by the Romans in 70 A.D., three boatloads of Jews were sent to Gaul, as France was then called. These sailors, traders, and physicians prospered. By the fifth century their descendants were also farmers and wine growers. A synagogue was established in Paris in 582. Between the eighth and ninth centuries, Charlemagne and his descendants gave Jews the same rights as Christians. Anyone who harmed Jews or their property was liable to drastic fines.

This co-existence was destroyed in 1096. The Crusaders, on their way to recapture Jerusalem from the Muslims,

sought out and attacked Jews, initiating centuries of persecution and anti-Semitism.

During the thirteenth century, 24 cartloads of the Talmud, the sacred Jewish interpretation of the laws of the Bible,
were burned. Jews were forced to wear yellow badges, to
single them out for further discrimination. In 1394, Jews were
expelled from France. For the next two hundred years, virtually no Jews lived in France.

By the French Revolution, however, there were 40,000
Jews living in France. Under Napoleon, they were accorded
full rights of citizenship. With the Age of Enlightenment, there
was greater religious tolerance. Judaism was recognized as a
religion, and the state paid rabbis' salaries, as it did for other
ministers.

It was therefore a shock when Alfred Dreyfus, a captain in the French Army, was falsely accused of selling military
secrets to the Germans in 1898. Cries of "death to the Jews"
rang throughout Paris. His trial reminded everyone that the
shallow grave of anti-Semitism was easily re-opened. Dreyfus
was convicted and given a life sentence to Devil's Island.
Despite a second trial, in which evidence was produced to
prove that Dreyfus had been framed, he was again found
guilty. A public protest followed, but it took twelve years for
the French courts to declare Dreyfus innocent.

By the twentieth century, Jews in France, as they had
elsewhere in Western Europe, had attained prominence and
prosperity. Leon Blum served as premier, and the Montpar-
nasse School of Artists included Marc Chagall and Amedeo
Modigliani.

By 1939, there were 350,000 Jews in France, many
refugees from other parts of Europe. When the German army
invaded Paris in 1940, most of the residents tried to flee. The
Germans forced them back. Unoccupied France, in the south,

was governed by the Vichy regime of Marshal Petain. He quickly abolished the Declaration of the Rights of Man and pledged to cooperate with the Germans.

French cooperation with the Germans was mixed. Many French citizens were sympathetic to the plight of native-born Jews. Some convents and monasteries hid children, and Protestant ministers were active in the rescue movements.

On October 4, 1940, the Vichy government agreed to the imprisonment of 25,000 Jewish refugees. They were placed in unheated barracks and given little food. A protest march by students was ignored.

At three a.m. on July 15, 1942, the French police, acting on German orders, knocked on the doors of foreign-born Jews. Thirteen thousand people were arrested. Men, women, and children were taken to a sweltering sports stadium and held without food or water for three days. Then they were deported to concentration camps.

After this, efforts to hide Jewish children increased. Many people housed refugees and didn't ask about their origins. One rescue group, operating near the city of Nancy, was responsible for helping over 6,000 prisoners escape from Paris to Spain.

Approximately 90,000 Jews from France perished at the hands of the Nazis.

A Bride in Name Only

Liliane Fould-Springer, the daughter of one of France's oldest and wealthiest Jewish families, should have been able to expect a fairy-tale existence when she became engaged to Elie de Rothschild, the son of Baron Robert de Rothschild. The Rothschilds were famous throughout the world for their vast financial empire, their friendship with royalty, their charitable foundations, and their service to their government. Instead, Liliane became a refugee, forced to flee, as were all Jews, from the Nazis.

MY mother warned me not to marry Elie de Rothschild. "Wait until the war is over," she said. "It's difficult enough being a Jew. As a Rothschild you'll be twice-hunted. The Germans would like nothing better than to hold the Rothschilds for ransom."

From the moment our country had declared war on Germany in September 1939, Elie had been awaiting his orders. How anxious he had been to serve France! His unit waited to be called up while the regular army sat on our borders, making no attempt to engage the Nazis in battle. For nine months we endured this phony war while Hitler conquered Poland, Lithuania, Estonia, and Norway. Then, on May 6, 1940, Elie's unit was mobilized, and I watched him canter off on horseback with the Eleventh Cavalry Regiment. How splendid he looked!

"We'll be married in September," he assured me. "The war will be over by then. In the meantime, I want you to stay with your family at the Château de Royamount, outside of Paris."

I busied myself helping on the estate. Except for the sixteen-year-old butler and the elderly chauffeur, the staff had

Elie de Rothschild, a member of the French Eleventh Cavalry Regiment, May 1940.

gone off to fight. We listened with growing apprehension to the news on the radio.

On May 10, 1940, we heard the worst. German parachutists had dropped into Holland. Belgium had been invaded. We were stunned. France would be next.

On May 28, 1940, the King of Belgium surrendered. British and French forces fighting on Belgian soil retreated to the northern coast of France where the beaches of Dunkirk were filled with every type of craft trying to evacuate the 300,000 Allied troops to England. If the soldiers were not evacuated, the troops would be decimated. I stood next to the radio, chilled. Was Elie alive?

Baron Robert de Rothschild, Elie's father, came from his nearby estate. "Look here, Liliane. You're a strong girl. We must hope for the best." He could hardly control the trembling in his voice. "We must leave here at once. You'll have to drive one of the cars. We'll meet again at the Château Lafite outside Bordeaux." He turned to the butler and the chauffeur. "You must drive the other two cars. Hurry everyone."

My nephew, David Pryce-Jones, who was four years old, darted towards the nursery. "I want my teddy!" he cried.

"No," the Baron said. "Hurry. . . ."

I ran to the library to fetch the family photograph albums, while the nannies, David, and my niece, Elena, squeezed into my car.

From the long driveway we could see a line of cars blowing their horns at pedestrians who clogged the roads. Some of the cars carried mattresses on their roofs. People moved along slowly with backpacks, suitcases, and sacks. One man led a goat; another carried a pair of squawking chickens. Many cars had been abandoned for lack of gasoline.

I tried to joke with the children. No one responded. David, whose mother had flown to England two weeks earlier to be with her husband, a British officer on leave, clutched my arm, his face pale. Where could I hide the children if we ran out of gasoline?

I took a back road, and three days later we reached the Château Lafite. The Baron was waiting in front of the iron gates of the mansion. He helped the children and their nannies out of the car and waited until they had started walking up to the house. Then he turned to me. "Liliane, the telephone is not working. You must go immediately and see your brother-in-law, Eduardo, in Bordeaux. He must get us visas to Spain or England." He thrust a large packet into my hands. "Here are the passports."

My oldest sister had married Eduardo Propper de Callejon, the Spanish Minister to Paris, now in Bordeaux. I had to reach him. The road to Bordeaux was even more jammed with refugees than the road out of Paris had been. Long lines circled the consulate. I could scarcely push my way through the door.

"I am the minister's sister-in-law," I shouted. "I must see him."

Eduardo stood at a card table stamping passports with both hands. He stopped to embrace me. "Go quickly, Liliane," he said after stamping all of our passports. "There's no time to lose."

I drove to the château in a turmoil. How had I suddenly become a refugee? My family had served France for generations. My great-uncle, Achille Fould, had been the Minister of Finance to Napoleon III. Now I was being hunted like a criminal. And what of Elie? Would I ever see him again?

"Thank God," said the Baron when I returned, "you have the visas. We are to leave on a British destroyer — my wife, my daughter, Cecile, and myself — to London. You must take the others across the border into Spain."

Once more, everyone climbed into the three cars. At the border we said goodbye to the chauffeur and butler. The Rolls Royce joined the other cars abandoned on the French side. Like a Pied Piper I led the frightened nannies and the children across the International Bridge at Hendage to Zaraz. It was not until I had everyone safe at the Grand Hotel at Zaraz that I collapsed.

For three months I lay in bed. I was devastated by the loss of my country and despondent over Elie. I assumed he must have been killed. My body broke out in boils and abcesses, and I retreated into my grief.

One miraculous day a Spanish friend of Eduardo's telephoned to tell me that Elie and his brother, Alain, were alive and prisoners of war in Germany. Within a few days the boils and abcesses vanished.

The first letter I received from Elie was typical. "The hell with Hitler. Let's marry just the same. I'll arrange a proxy wedding in prison. Go to Vichy and do the same."

A proxy wedding? Proxy weddings were arranged when either the bride or the groom could not be present. They were not uncommon in wartime. I would have to go to a magistrate and take my vows alone.

I wrote to my mother who was in Canada. "I know that you wanted a grand wedding in the Great Synagogue of Paris after the war, but Elie feels that, if we marry by proxy, it could save my life. As the wife of a French officer, I would be put in a special camp rather than rounded up with the other Jews."

She protested, thinking that by my *not* marrying Elie, I would have a better chance for survival. The Vichy government objected for different reasons. They refused to grant me permission to marry a French officer because I was Jewish.

The German government had no objections. In October 1941, Elie, in the presence of a German and a French

Liliane Fould-Springer at her proxy wedding to Elie de Rothschild. Note the empty chair next to her.

general, said his vows from prison. It was not until April 1942 that I was able to obtain similar permission. At Cannes, I stood beside an empty chair and pledged myself to Elie de Rothschild. The magistrate who performed the civil ceremony did not offer his congratulations.

Eduardo was now in Tangier. He had been demoted because he had issued visas too freely. I joined him and my sister in North Africa.

Elie's letter acknowledging the news of the proxy wedding reached me there. "Some day, my darling, we shall live together as man and wife, and *soon.*"

I knew, from the wording of the letter, that he might attempt an escape. I returned to France so that I could be with him if he did. My brother, Max Fould-Springer, obtained false papers for me. There was little to eat in the south of France except fish and olives. Many nights I lay awake, my head and stomach aching from hunger.

Word reached me that Elie's attempt to escape had failed. The Germans had moved him deeper into Germany to Colditz Castle in Saxony, a maximum security prison.

My brother insisted that we leave France immediately for Spain. We were to meet in Marseilles at the Hotel Terminus to obtain another set of false papers. As I stood at the desk to register, Max came up behind me. "Go to the door on my left," he said quietly. He had noticed that the lobby was filled with German officers. "Go immediately to the Spanish consul."

At the Spanish consulate we saw storm troopers guarding all the entrances. We later found out that the Germans had seized Vichy the night before. Without stopping, I hurried to the railroad station and boarded a center car without the new set of papers. I hoped the guards would begin their inspection of passports at either end, and I would be safe by the time my turn came.

Elie de Rothschild after his capture, in prison camp (January 1941).

My heart fell to the floor when a young soldier entered my car. I took out my comb and pretended to freshen my hair.

"Your passport please, Fraulein," said the squat, dark-haired soldier, looking tired and homesick. "Have a good journey," he said, returning my fake passport.

From Spain we flew to Morocco, and I remained there until 1944. I flew back to Paris on Liberation Day, August 25, 1944. I stood on the Champs-Elysées as General de Gaulle strode through the Arc de Triomphe. My joy for my country's freedom was overwhelming. But my heart still ached. I had had no word from Elie. Would I remain a bride in name only . . . a widow before I was even a wife?

For seven months we tried to find out if Elie and Alain were safe. In May 1945, we received news that they were alive.

A few weeks later, with both bride and groom present, Liliane Fould-Springer and Elie de Rothschild were remarried in a quiet religious ceremony in the Great Synagogue of Paris.

The Baron and Baroness Elie de Rothschild live in Paris. She is a recognized authority on art, as well as a photographer and interior designer, and the only woman member of the Conseil des Musees de France (which oversees the museums of France). The French government has awarded her the Legion of Honor and made her an Officer of Arts and Letters. She has 3 children and several grandchildren.

Tunnels

Rene Gallant's nightmare began in Paris when she was ten. Her father, a member of the French Resistance, was arrested. Three years later, her mother was taken in the round-up of French Jews.

When I met her in Israel and asked her to tell me of her experiences, she said, "I cry every time I talk about it. But I will talk to you."

I listened and cried with her.

115

I AM IN A TUNNEL, ON MY KNEES. I SEE A SMALL LIGHT VERY, VERY FAR AWAY, BUT I CANNOT STAND UP. I HAVE TO CRAWL ON MY KNEES. IF I WANT TO CONTINUE, THERE ARE BIG BLACK CATS THAT I HAVE TO HOLD IN MY HANDS AND KILL. IT TAKES HOURS AND HOURS — HOURS WITHOUT END.

I don't remember when I started having that dream, but the dream is very clear. I can close my eyes and see myself holding a cat, two feet in one hand, two feet in the other and breaking its spine. In front of me, an endless column of black cats. I have to break all their spines. Even today, the dream still haunts me.

When I was ten years old, I watched the blonde German troops goose-step down the Champs-Elysées. How handsome they looked! I could not associate them with the ranting, shouting man named Hitler that I had heard on the radio.

I went to school as usual, although I played with my friends with a gas mask slung over one shoulder and a Star of David sewn on the other.

My father, who had been a member of the Resistance, was arrested in 1941 and imprisoned at Drancy. In 1942, he was sent with the first shipment of French Jews to Auschwitz.

February 1943 was very cold. With my mother and brothers and sister, I sat wrapped in a blanket, puzzling over my lessons.

There was a knock at the door. "Gestapo, open up!"

My mother had prepared me for her arrest. She picked up a small bundle she had kept packed, kissed the four of us

Round up of foreign-born Jews in France during the Nazi occupation.

goodbye, and left. I ran to the window and watched her get into the van. Even today, I tremble when I hear the piercing sound of a police alarm.

Now I was responsible for my two brothers and three-year-old sister. I was thirteen. I took Mother's heavy dress from the closet and ripped open the hem in which she had sewn gold pieces. I put the money into a cloth bag along with our identity cards and important papers. I pinned the bag to my underpants.

"Rene," my mother had told me again and again, "unless someone undresses you or you are arrested, no one can take that bag from you."

When my sister woke up crying, I held her on my lap and rocked her back and forth. A Christian neighbor knocked on the door. "The grocer says not to worry. He will save milk for you. You don't have to stand in line at eight a.m."

Another neighbor brought us a bag filled with pieces of leather.

"Here is work for you. Put the loops, one through the other, to make belts," he said.

The two boys and I sat on the floor and pushed one loop through the other while the baby played with the pieces under the dining-room table. When we were finished, the neighbor paid us a few cents each for the 12,000 belts we had made.

Every night I would fall into bed exhausted. The dream of the tunnel and the cats would awaken me. I realized I had to have help. How long could a thirteen-year-old girl cope with a toddler and two young boys?

The Jewish Council arranged for the children to board with a farmer in Normandy. I stayed in the apartment alone, each creak in the floor reminding me of the children's laughter. I went out only to buy food. At night I would awaken, exhausted, my hands limp and aching from the recurring nightmare of the black cats.

When I could no longer stand it, I went to a Jewish organization that promised to smuggle me into Palestine. "Two men will come and take you to the underground," they said.

One morning I left my fourth-floor apartment. Two men stopped me on the second-floor landing. "Does Mademoiselle Gallant live here?"

Jews or the Gestapo? "No," I said automatically. "She doesn't live here."

When I returned from the grocers, the concierge stopped me. "The Gestapo came for you."

Where could I go? Some non-Jewish Russians lived across the street. I knocked at their door. "The Gestapo came to fetch me. I don't know where to go."

The frightened woman pulled me inside. "Take off your star and burn it. Two men have been watching this street."

The next morning, as I was braiding my hair, I looked in the mirror and saw the woman standing beside me, holding my coat. "I'm sorry," she told me, "it is too dangerous to keep you. You must leave."

I wandered through Paris not knowing what to do. Finally, exhausted from the cold and fear, I ignored the "No Jews and Dogs Allowed" sign at the Jardin des Tuileries and brushed aside the snow to sit on a park bench. Who would take me in? Friends, relatives . . . a ghost list.

I walked past the Seine, wondering if the answer would be to jump into the river. No! Someday I would be reunited with my family. Somehow, I found myself at the home of some Jewish friends. Fifteen refugees were crowded around their dining-room table. Two of them had escaped from the concentration camp called Auschwitz.

The host refused to believe their story. "Maybe they are killing people, but not the way you describe, with pits and with ovens. The Germans are not that barbaric. This is 1943." All of us nodded. These Poles must either be mistaken or crazy.

The next morning, I got on the subway. Without the Star, I could no longer sit in the Jewish car. In the first-class section, two German officers tapped my shoulder. I froze, my hand clamped to the overhead strap. They were going to arrest me.

"Mademoiselle, please take my seat," the tall one said. I shook my head, hearing only the pounding in my heart. "But you must sit down. A pretty girl should not have to stand."

I nodded and forced myself to move into the seat. I continued on by train to Normandy. As long as I had money, the farmer who was housing my brothers and sister allowed me to stay. I milked the cows, tidied the house and did chores. As soon as the money was gone, the farmer told me to leave.

I trudged ten miles through the snow to the train station. I dozed through the ride, too exhausted to think. I dreamed of the tunnel and the black cats.

After the liberation of France, members of the National Resistance Movement marched through Paris.

When I awakened, I was in Paris. With my last pennies, I bought a ticket for the subway. Tears poured down my frost-bitten cheeks as I sat on the platform and watched the trains go by. The cats had won. I hardly noticed the woman standing next to me. She kept looking up and down the platform.

Finally, when no one was around, she sat down beside me. "Are you Jewish?"

"Yes," I said, too desperate to care.

"I'm Jewish, too. Come with me." She and her sister and daughter lived in an apartment near the Louvre, with false identity papers. Though they treated me like a servant, they invited me to use their library. There, in the most savage of times, I would curl up in a chair and share the companionship of the greatest philosophers.

August 1944! The Germans abandoned Paris. I stood on the Champs-Elysées, the site of the Arc de Triomphe, close enough to touch General de Gaulle and General Le Clerc as they led the victory parade. Cheering, crying, jumping with joy, I was filled with new life.

I left my benefactors and took many jobs to support myself. The Jewish agency insisted I could not care for my brothers and sister properly and placed them with Jewish families.

On November 29, 1947, I stood in front of a radio shop listening to the loudspeaker as members of the United Nations voted on the partitioning of Palestine. Fifty-six countries voted "aye." At the end, the announcer declared, "The State of Israel is created."

I looked at my reflection in the shop window. Something very special had happened. Somehow, I had grown taller. I turned to the stranger behind me. "Can you tell?" I asked proudly.

"Tell what?"

"I'm Jewish. I have a state!"

Rene fought in the Israeli War of Independence of 1948. She lives in Haifa with her husband and two children.

HUNGARY

Six hundred years before Magyar horsemen swept out of Asia and across southeastern Europe into Dacia, or ancient Hungary, settlements of Jews existed among the rolling Hungarian plains. The Magyars, who were pagans, conquered the territory in 895. A hundred years later, they became Christians. At first Jews were tolerated. It was not until the thirteenth century that restrictive measures were taken against Jews. The right of Jews to own property was revoked, and they were forced to wear special badges.

Increasing pressure by the Pope initiated the first expulsion of Jews from Hungary in 1349. The edict was revoked and Jews returned, only to be expelled again in 1360. Four years later, they were permitted to return.

When the Turks captured Hungary in 1526, they allowed Jews civil and religious freedom. These liberties were taken away when the Hapsburg Dynasty of Austria conquered the Turks in 1686. The new Catholic rulers expelled the Jews. When Jews were at last permitted to return, they were heavily taxed for the privilege of living in Hungary.

In 1867 Hungary became autonomous under an Austrian-Hungarian monarch and Jews were accorded citizens' rights. Anti-Semitism, however, continued to flourish. Jewish merchants were boycotted. By 1920, the number of Jews allowed to work in the professions, hold public office, or go to universities was limited. During the 1930's, the Hungarian government followed a Nazi-like policy towards Jews and imposed many restrictive measures. Still, most Hungarian Jews deluded themselves into thinking these anti-Semitic measures were temporary.

At the beginning of the war Hungary was allied with Germany. Young Jewish men were used in labor battalions to work on roads and to clear mine fields. Nevertheless the Hungarian regent, Admiral Horthy, resisted Hitler's demands to cooperate in the total elimination of Hungarian Jews.

In 1944, with the defeat of the Germans a real possibility, Horthy sought a peace settlement with the Allies. Hitler, furious, sent his troops into Hungary. Adolf Eichmann arrived with the troops to oversee personally the extermination of the Hungarian Jews. The round-ups began and the trains, filled with Jews of all ages, began to roll towards Auschwitz.

Jewish leaders pleaded with the Allies to destroy the railroad tracks and bridges leading to Auschwitz to slow down the deportations to the death camp. The Allies refused to divert planes for that purpose.

When the German Minister of Home Defense, Heinrich Himmler, ordered a halt to the killing of the Jews, the Hungarian Fascist Organization, the Arrow Cross, vowed to complete the total destruction of Hungarian Jews. "We shall destroy every Jew in Hungary so they cannot serve as witnesses," they declared. The massacres continued even after the arrival of Allied Russian troops.

Of the 750,000 pre-war Hungarian Jewish population, approximately 200,000 died in the prison camps or were murdered.

The Masquerade

Ilona was ten when she first experienced Nazi anti-Semitism. Her comfortable life in Budapest was never the same.

IT was the Sabbath before Passover in 1933. Thousands of Jews were gathered near the Dohanyi Street Synagogue, the largest in Europe, waving to friends and enjoying the pleasant spring weather.

I walked inside the sanctuary and looked to see if the Eternal Light hanging over the Ark was still burning. I sat next to Laszlo, my brother, who was to be bar mitzvahed the next month. I adored him.

The Great Rabbi of all Hungary, Simon Hevesi, entered and the cantor began the hymn: "Come oh Sabbath Day and bring peace and healing on thy wing . . ."

Suddenly two pistol shots rang out. My brother pushed me to the floor and covered me with his body. I heard a rabbi say, "Please, everyone remain seated."

Two more shots rang out. People screamed. A younger rabbi calmly walked down the steps nearest the gunman. He knocked the two pistols out of the assassin's hands as others grabbed him.

"Please return to your seats. The service will continue." Rabbi Hevesi began to read the opening prayer.

It was my first experience with anti-Semitism. Life for Hungarian Jews had been pleasant. Even in 1938, when the laws restricting businesses were passed, my father's position was unaffected. He managed an industrial plant, and his bosses merely moved his desk to the back room.

My brother was drafted into the army the same year. In 1940, he and other Jewish soldiers were taken out of their regular units and sent to clear minefields.

I graduated from high school in 1942. I was nineteen. My friends and I celebrated at an ice-cream parlor overlooking the Danube River. Gypsy music from the cafe next door drifted out into the streets. Even though the rest of Europe was in turmoil, Budapest was filled with young couples sitting on benches along the tree-lined streets and children munching pastries from the sweet shops.

Although I had not been allowed to enter medical school (I had graduated with highest honors), I was allowed to go to the university as a psychology student.

In December 1942, I received a letter from Laszlo. "My outfit is being sent to the Ukrainian front. Please come and say farewell."

I knew I must go, even though Jews had been forbidden to ride on trains. I dressed in a drab, dark coat and a shawl, and tied a babushka over my curly hair. Mother packed two huge baskets with meats and pastries. I boarded a third-class car, praying no one would recognize me. The train was cold and damp.

It was storming when the train pulled into the station. I trudged through the heavy snowfall to the base, arriving just as the soldiers were being loaded onto the trucks.

"Have you seen Laszlo Miklosh?" I asked.

A big fat Hungarian colonel seized me by the shoulders. "What are you doing here?"

"I am looking for my brother. I have traveled all day to say goodbye."

The colonel pulled off my babushka. His hand crept across my hair to my neck, then to my shoulders, then below. "You can see him if you promise to go to bed with me."

I shuddered. "Yes," I whispered.

"Hey," he called to two guards. "Help this Jew find her brother, then make sure she returns. Give her fifteen minutes."

He turned to me and caught my throat in one hand. "If you're fooling me, I'll kill you."

We walked through the falling snow from wagon to wagon calling out my brother's name. Finally, he jumped out of one of the convoys, wearing only pants and an undershirt.

I wrapped my wet shawl around him and wept. "Where is your warm coat and the heavy sweater I knitted for you?"

"The guards took all our outer garments and blankets." He stood there, trying not to shiver. I kissed him. My golden-haired brother had become a wrinkled old man.

"What shall I do about the colonel, Laszlo?"

"Tell the soldiers you left some apples in the station and that you will bring them back in a few minutes." He hugged me goodbye.

The station was dark and empty. I hid in a wooden crib. Between the chinks I saw the two soldiers storm into the station. Their boots stamped across the wooden floor as they searched for me. When they left I went inside, cold and shaking, and fell asleep under a bench.

The next morning I took the train back to Budapest. For three days I lay in bed, trembling with fever and fear, afraid to tell anyone what had happened.

On March 19, 1944, Eichmann came to Budapest. All Jews were ordered to wear the Yellow Star. I carefully measured the distance from my shoulder to my heart. Those with "improperly" sewn stars were stopped and deported.

It was no longer safe to go to school. My father had long since been dismissed from his job. One night, a plumber knocked at our door. "The landlord sent me to fix the pipes. Show me what is wrong," he said, bringing his tool box into the house.

I stared at him. It was Ferencz, a former rabbinical student. "The Arrow Cross is after your father," he said quietly.

Father picked up his jacket and walked out the door.

Instead of ringing for the elevator, he walked downstairs and hid behind the palm plants in the lobby. Several Hungarian Nazis were questioning the doorman.

"We know Mr. Miklosh is in this building. He is not to leave or you will pay with your life." They entered the elevator. The doorman beckoned to my father to leave. He then turned his back and bent down as if to straighten a piece of carpet.

Father fled to an abandoned movie studio and caught a terrible cold sleeping on the damp floor. He went to a hospital run by an American doctor. A few nights later a Jewish man, whom everyone suspected of working with the Nazis, came by.

"I was worried about your whereabouts," he told Father. "I'm glad to find you well. Let me know if you need anything."

That evening the Gestapo appeared at Father's bedside. "Come with us."

The head of the hospital entered the room. "You're wasting your time," he told the Gestapo. "This man is very ill; he will be dead by morning. I swear on my life."

The Nazis left. The doctor notified Ferencz who took my father to another hideaway, the home of a retired Hungarian colonel.

I began to help Ferencz falsify documents. We used diluted chlorox to change dates. Care had to be taken not to discolor the paper and to duplicate the exact pressure of the lettering.

When the air raid alarms sounded on June 6, 1944 — D-Day — I climbed to the roof and watched American planes score a direct hit on the oil refineries on the edge of the city. Jagged skyscrapers of flames, first red and gold and then black, raged through the sky.

A week later the entire Jewish community was ordered

to move to "Star Houses." Yellow stars were painted on the gates and the doors of the apartments. Mother and I crowded into a small three-room unit with two other families.

One day Ferencz came to the apartment and told us to hide. A friend we had arranged to stay with had no more room. She rented space for us next door, and we moved in with two strangers. They began to question us.

Mother was nervous. I spoke up. "We are running away from the Russians. They came to our village and took our cows and tried to rape us."

Mother began to cry. The man, glancing at Mother's soft hands, excused himself. When the girl went into the kitchen, I called a taxi.

As the taxi pulled away, we saw a police van stop in front of the building. We reached the home of a cousin who had married a Gentile. They were on their way to an air raid shelter.

"We'll stay in your apartment," Mother whispered, "so no one will know you have guests."

One night I woke up in a sweat. I kept dreaming I heard the sound of gunfire. I opened the window. In the moonlight I saw long lines of naked people being whipped and driven towards the Danube. The icy edges of the river turned red as the bodies dropped into the "blue" Danube.

The next morning we learned that one of the homes under the protection of the Swiss and Swedish embassies had been raided by the Arrow Cross, the Hungarian Nazis.

Our cousins, frightened, told us to leave. Where could we go? A Christian friend gave us a room in her house.

One night, when the bombing was more intense than usual, Mother suggested we move the bed away from the window and put the piano there instead. We managed to move the furniture with a great deal of tugging and sat down to rest. Minutes later a shell splintered the piano.

Ferencz found us again. "It is not safe for you. I will take you to your father's hiding place."

We climbed into the back of his truck and drove to the apartment. More than forty-five people were crowded into a blacked-out basement. They had not dared to go outside for several months.

It was not until February 13, 1945, when the fighting finally ceased, that it was safe for a Jew to walk through the streets. I passed the synagogue on Csaky Street; it had been used by the Arrow Cross as stables.

Rabbi Josef Berkovics, dressed in his robes, stood there arguing with a Russian sergeant who had come to take over the building.

"This is a House of God. It cannot be used for profane purposes."

The soldier shrugged and went away. The rabbi and a few helpers began to shovel out the filth and scour the walls. That evening there was a sign on the door: "Prayer Services: Morning — 7 a.m.; Evening — 5:10 p.m."

The Jewish community, which had been in Hungary since Roman times, had endured.

Ilona is married and now lives in the United States.

PALESTINE

Anti-Semitism did not end when the Axis forces surrendered. Jews, who had survived the camps and those who had emerged from hiding, attempted to return to their homes.

Some found their villages had been destroyed. Friends and families had been annihilated. Their neighbors, who had seized the homes and businesses of Jewish citizens, greeted the survivors with hostility. "It's a pity that Hitler didn't get a chance to finish the job," was a not uncommon "welcome." It was better to move on, to make a life elsewhere.

The refugees turned towards the displaced-persons camps established by the Allies. President Harry S. Truman ordered the borders of Germany and Austria open to any refugee wishing to leave Europe.

For months, the survivors poured into the displaced-persons camps in the hope of eventually reaching Palestine, which was under British jurisdiction. The British refused to let the refugees in. They remained in the camps, ignored by the rest of the world.

B'riha, an underground movement that had been organized by soldiers of the Jewish Brigade of the British 8th Army, began to smuggle Jews out of Eastern Europe into Palestine. Some refugees were led on foot over the Alps into Italy. Others were transported in "borrowed" British trucks across the Communist-held borders of Eastern Europe to temporary shelters in Italy. From there, they were taken to Mediterranean ports, such as Marseilles and Venice, and put aboard illegal ships. These illegal ships were often intercepted by the British and temporarily detained on Cyprus.

Nevertheless, one thousand members of B'riha spirited a half million Jews out of Europe and into Palestine.

Flight to Freedom

Eytan Bar-on was born in Haifa but went to Europe in 1939 when he was eleven years old. At fourteen, he became a fugitive from the Gestapo.

THE day of my father's execution, I stood in the shadows of the town hall and waited for him to be brought outside. When he emerged, handcuffed to two Gestapo agents, I sauntered across the empty square. Our eyes met. I was fourteen years old and I loved him very much.

We had gone to Europe in 1939 because my mother needed an operation. While she was recuperating in Switzerland, my father took my sister and me to visit relatives in France. When the war started we were not permitted to leave.

My father had been a British secret service agent in Palestine. I knew nothing of his activities in France, but he must have contacted the French underground. One morning two men came to my school, spoke to the teacher, and took my sister and me outside. It was October 1942.

As the four of us walked down the street, the two men suddenly pushed us against a wall and hid us. I peeked out to see my father handcuffed between two Gestapo agents. He passed very close by. He saw me clearly.

The next day I saw a poster in the town square. "Monsieur Bar-on has been arrested for underground activities." A few days later another poster appeared. "The spy, Bar-on, will be shot on Tuesday."

After his death, the Resistance sent my sister in one direction, me in another. They feared we, too, would be arrested. For three years staying alive became a game.

I slept in barns, haystacks, caves. Sometimes I ate turnips and potatoes. Sometimes I didn't have anything to eat. I became a messenger for the underground. Looking back, I realize how foolish I was. I took unnecessary risks: When

Members of B'riha helping Jewish survivors to escape to Palestine.

distributing underground literature, I would go into a street-car and slip the pamphlets into the pockets of German soldiers.

I can't recall all the places I hid. I finally ended up near the Spanish border. The underground was trying to smuggle a group of us over the Pyrenees into Spain. Three times we had to return to our hiding places. Finally we were put into trucks and passed through the checkpoint; I think a lot of money must have changed hands.

From Spain, the British ambassador (since we were British subjects) managed to smuggle us aboard a ship at Gibraltar for Palestine.

Our house in Palestine, in the hills of Carmel, was filled with strangers. I joined the *Hachshara,* a movement for young people to establish new *kibbutzim* and to develop the *Haganah,* a Jewish underground.

My group was called the *Palmach* division. We were to smuggle in arms and hide illegal immigrants. The British did not allow Jews to carry arms. The Jews were stopped on streets and buses and searched.

One day, when we had arms hidden in our truck, we were stopped at the checkpoint. "What's in the box?" a soldier asked, pointing to a large box we were sitting on.

"It's just a seat," we answered.

He pulled up the top, exposing mortars. None of us was over seventeen, but possession of arms was punishable by death. Would I be shot like my father?

We were sentenced to seven years in jail and sent to Acco, a medieval fortress. It is not a pleasant place to spend one's youth. Luckily, we were freed in ten days.

At the end of World War II, the Palmach sent me to Europe to work with children who had survived the Holocaust. Children from Buchenwald were brought in trucks to a camp near Marseilles. They had never really been allowed to be children. Some had been used in medical experiments. They regarded everyone with suspicion. When offered chocolate by American soldiers, they would refuse. Only bread was valued. They stuffed it in their socks, in their underwear. They slept with it under their pillows and stole it from the dining room. Could the kibbutz movement ever rebuild their souls?

On my return to Palestine, I continued my work with the Palmach. In 1947, the United Nations voted to partition Palestine into Jewish and Arab states. The Arabs attacked. Now we battled to control the roads and to allow the Jewish settlements to grow and flourish. When the Arabs cut off the road to Jerusalem, I was one of the soldiers who ran the blockade. On one trip I was wounded, and it was not until a few months before the end of the war that I could rejoin the troops.

The day the final armistice was signed, July 20, 1949, I realized I had been a soldier since I was fourteen, in the underground or on the battlefield. After ten years of fighting, how did one enjoy peace?

I flirted with girls and hung out at the beach. I entered the university but found the classroom stifling. I took a job and educated myself by reading anything I could find in Hebrew, English, and French.

I continued to work with the army during the Arab-Israeli wars and served as an interpreter for foreign journalists.

The story of my life — the life of a Palestinian Jew — is marked by the blood of my father and my people. I have never known a decade of peace, yet I believe it is possible. The days of our exodus are over.

Eytan Bar-on is employed by an Israeli shipping firm. He, his wife and four children are "sabras", native-born Israelis.

Glossary

Allies — an alliance formed to fight Germany and Italy (and later Japan). Originally included: Great Britain, France, Canada, Australia, New Zealand, and South Africa. The United States and the Soviet Union joined later.

anti-Semitism — hatred towards or discrimination of Jews.

Aryan — a pseudo-scientific term based on 19th century racial and linguistic theories used by the Nazis and others to describe a superior or "master" race, i.e. white Europeans, specifically Germans. The idealized Aryan was blond, blue-eyed, and healthy. The Jewish or "Semitic" race was considered inferior and evil.

Ashkenazis — Jews of German origin.

Auschwitz — (Oswiecim in Polish) The group of Nazi concentration camps built in 1940 near Kracow, Poland. It included the extermination camp at Birkenau where more than 2½ million people, mostly Polish Jews, were killed, mainly in gas chambers.

banzai — a Japanese shout or cheer, used especially among combat troops when attacking.

Bar Mitzvah — a Jewish ceremony in which a young man, usually at the age of 13, assumes adult responsibilities. The term means "Son of the Commandment." A similar ceremony for girls is the Bat Mitzvah.

Bismarck, Otto von — Prussian statesman who forged the individual German states into one empire in the late 19th century.

bounty hunters — those who hunt in return for a premium or reward, such as money, especially one offered by the government.

boycott — a refusal to do business and prevent others from doing business with a person, group of people, company, or country.

Buchenwald — one of the earliest concentration camps, established in 1937, to hold political enemies of the Nazis. More than 200,000 people died at Buchenwald.

Champs-Elysées — main boulevard in Paris, site of the Arc de Triomphe.

concierge — (French) custodian, janitor.

Cossacks — peasant-soldiers in the Ukraine and several regions of Russia, first formed in the 15th century.

Crystal Night — a nationwide riot on November 9 and 10, 1938, directed against the Jews in Germany. It is called Crystal Night because of the shattered glass windows of shops, synagogues, and homes.

Dachau — concentration camp in Germany near the town of Dachau, ten miles from Munich, built in 1933 as a camp for Jews and political prisoners. More than 40,000 people were killed there.

Eichmann, Adolf Otto (1906-1945) — Nazi leader and head of propaganda, who was among the initiators of the "Final Solution."

ersatz — (German) inferior substitute.

Final Solution — term used by the Nazis to describe their plan for the annihilation or destruction of the entire Jewish people through mass murder by shooting, gassing, or starvation.

Führer — (German) leader. Adolf Hitler adopted the title when he rose to power.

gefilte fish — made from chopped, boneless fish such as whitefish, carp, or pike and shaped into balls or sticks.

Gentile — in ancient times, and in the Bible, the term means any non-Jew. Today the word is sometimes used to mean Christian.

Gestapo — secret police force of Nazi Germany. The name is a short form of *Geheime Staatspolizei* (secret state police). The Nazi party used the Gestapo, noted for its power and brutality, to smash opposition.

guerrilla — a member of an independent unit carrying out irregular warfare, such as harassment and sabotage.

Himmler, Heinrich (1900-1945) — Nazi leader and one of Hitler's chief assistants. He became head of the SS in 1929 and of the German police in 1936; later assumed overall responsibility for the total destruction of Jews in Europe when the SS was put in charge of the "Final Solution."

Hitler, Adolf (1889-1945) — Austrian-born founder and leader of the Nazi party who ruled Germany as dictator from 1933-1945. He began his rise to power in 1919 and outlined his plans to re-establish the glory of pre-World War I Germany by conquering Europe and expelling or eliminating the Jews in his book, *Mein Kampf* (My Life).

Heil Hitler — (German) Hail, Hitler.

Hitler Youth — Nazi youth organization to indoctrinate German youth.

Iron Cross — Germany's first and highest decoration for military valor, created by King Friedrich Wilhelm III in 1813.

Kaiser — title used by rulers of the German Empire. Kaiser is the German form of the Latin word caesar (emperor). Kaisers ruled Germany from 1871-1918.

kapos — prisoners in concentration camps who were chosen by the SS to make sure that other prisoners performed the work assigned to them. In camps that were mostly Jewish, the Germans appointed Jewish kapos.

kibbutz — a mainly agricultural community in Israel based on the collective ownership and control of labor and property.

Kraut — (slang) an uncomplimentary name meaning "German."

Majdanek — concentration and extermination camp in Lublin, Poland, established in 1941. About 125,000 Jews perished there.

Marranos — Spanish and Portuguese Jews forcibly converted to Christianity in the 14th and 15th centuries. They continued to practice Judaism in secret.

Nazi — political party, *Nationalsozialistiche Deutsche Arbeiterparei* (National Socialist German Workers' Party). The word *Nazi* stands for the first word of the party.

partisans — those working behind enemy lines in wartime to undermine the opponent's hold on their homeland and to support military operations of their allies. See *resistance, underground*.

Passover — (Hebrew) Pesach. A spring festival commemorating the exodus of the Jews from Egypt and slavery, highlighted by the *seder* (see below).

pogrom — (Russian word) organized massacre against defenseless people.

Reichstag — German parliament.

Resistance — underground (secret) movement in a conquered country to sabotage and defeat the occupying powers. See *partisans, underground*.

scapegoat — someone who is blamed for another's misdeeds or misfortune.

seder — (Hebrew) order, or order of service. The ceremony or services which mark the observance of Passover. Included are special or symbolic foods relating to Jewish history and religion, and a retelling of the exodus or escape of Jews out of Egypt and slavery.

Sephardic — Jews of Spanish or Portuguese origin.

shabbas goy — a non-Jew who performs household tasks for religious Jews on the Sabbath day when they are prohibited, by religious law, from doing any work, such as turning on an electric light.

shtetls — Eastern European villages of Jewish settlers.

SS — (German) abbreviation for *Schutzstaffel*. Originally Hitler's bodyguards; later they became Nazi security and intelligence personnel.

Staatsopera — German state opera.

storm troopers — private army or police organized byHitler when he began his rise to power. Armed with guns, they protected Nazi rallies and fought anyone who tried to break up Nazi gatherings.

swastika — ancient symbol, used by several cultures, as an ornament or religious sign. It was adapted in 1920 as the symbol of the Nazi party.

synagogue — Jewish house of worship.

Talmud — collection of books containing treatises on Jewish law, regulations, traditions, customs, rites, ceremonies, civil and criminal law.

Third Reich — official name of the Nazi government, meaning the third empire.

underground — an illegal and secret movement to resist occupying powers or to obtain a political goal. See *resistance, partisans, guerilla*.

Wannsee Conference — held on January 20, 1942, near Berlin at which plans for the "Final Solution" — the extermination of all Jews — were approved by the Nazis.

Warsaw Ghetto — area in Warsaw, Poland, in which 500,000 Jews were confined by the Germans until they could be shipped to concentration camps. In an uprising in April 1943, poorly armed Jews battled German tanks for weeks before the ghetto was wiped out.

Weimar Republic — democratic German government established after World War I, overthrown in the early 1930s by the Nazis.

Yellow Star (of David) — Jews through the ages have often been forced to wear badges or other symbols to identify themselves. The six-pointed star or hexagram known as the *Magen David* (Hebrew: Shield of David) became recognized from the 17th century on as a symbol of Jewish national identity.

Yeshiva — a school where rabbis are trained and the Talmud and other literature are studied.

Yiddish — a language which is a mixture of German and Hebrew.

Youth Aliyah — Zionist movement to train young people for immigration to Palestine.

Zionism — movement to establish Palestine (now Israel) as the national Jewish homeland.

Index